I HEARD THE VOICE OF GOD

A short testimony of God's call to the ministry

S. S. Peter, Th.D., Ph.D.

WESTBOW
PRESS®
A DIVISION OF THOMAS NELSON
& ZONDERVAN

WestBow Press books may be ordered through booksellers or by contacting:

WestBow Press
A Division of Thomas Nelson & Zondervan
1663 Liberty Drive
Bloomington, IN 47403
www.westbowpress.com
844-714-3454

Scripture taken from the King James Version of the Bible.

ISBN: 978-1-6642-3235-8 (sc)
ISBN: 978-1-6642-3236-5 (e)

Print information available on the last page.

WestBow Press rev. date: 5/12/2021

Contents

Dedication

This book is dedicated primarily to my
Savior and Lord Jesus Christ.

Secondly, I dedicate this book to all the readers.

Acknowledgment

First of all, I want to thank the Lord for inspiring me to put together this book. I would not have been able to get this done without God's grace.

Then I want to express my special appreciation to my son for typing the manuscript as well as organizing and editing it.

I am also grateful to my wife for suggestions, help and facilitating the publishing of the book.

Introduction

Today, many people don't believe in God. Then there are many who believe Jesus as their personal Savior. However, some don't believe that He heals the sick and does miracles today.

In this book, I have written about some of the healings and miracles that I have experienced in my own life and witnessed in my ministry, as we read in Hebrews 2:4, "God also bearing them witness, both with signs and wonders, and with divers miracles, and gifts of the Holy Ghost, according to his own will."

I hope this book will encourage readers to trust in God, not only for their salvation, but also for their healing and deliverance.

one

꿰

PRAYER ANSWERED

I was born in a Christian family. My father was a mission school teacher. When he got married, he was wishing for a son, but he got two daughters. He was disappointed. Then he prayed for a son. I was the first son, and after that seven more sons were born. All together, we were eight sons and two daughters. Soon after I was born, the second sister who was about two years old died. My father felt very sad and guilty that he was disappointed when his daughters were born. He wrote a song about her and sang, playing a banjo, to express his grief over her death.

When I was born, I was a healthy baby. My father tested my eyes and my hearing, and everything was perfect. Forty days after my birth, my eyes closed for some reason, and I could not open my eyes. Even though they tried to open my eyes, I could not see anything. My father started worrying and thinking, "God gave me a son, and now he is blind." He tried everything, but nothing worked. Finally, he humbled himself, kneeled down, prayed, and asked God to open my eyes. He said, "Lord, if you open the eyes of my son, I will fast every Friday until I die." As soon as he finished his prayer and said, "Amen," I opened my eyes. So, I can say I was blind, literally blind, and now I can see. Praise God.

MY INTRODUCTION TO CHRISTIANITY

I was learning from the beginning what my father was teaching me about Christianity. He was telling me Jesus Christ is the only God, and He is the God of the universe. I was born and raised in India. There are so many religions and so many gods in India. They say they have 33 million gods, but I was so proud that we have a God and His name is Jesus. I was not born again, I was not saved. I went to a Hindu school, and every morning they would have Hindu prayer and Hindu teaching about their gods. I didn't want to learn about their gods, because their stories didn't make any sense to me. I tried to skip that first hour and go a little bit late to school. I was the only student who was late to school, and the headmaster gave me so much beating on my hands that my hands were swelling. So, I started attending their morning prayer and Hindu teaching. The more I learned about Hinduism, the more I disliked it. I appreciated that Jesus Christ was not an idol, but He is a real God. I was telling everybody about Jesus Christ, but there was no born again experience in my life.

I was a bright student in my class, and I was studying very well. I didn't care that I was blind and now I could see. That was just like a story, I never paid attention. I never thought of what the born again experience was all about because we were nominal Christians. We didn't know anything about the born again experience. Whatever my father learned from the Bible, he was teaching me and telling me, but he did not know how to tell someone to get saved.

I was regularly going to Sunday school and learning about Christianity, but I didn't learn too much in Sunday school, because my father taught me more than what I was learning in Sunday school. I was very active in church, taking part in dramas. I was writing Christian songs and singing. So the elders of the church tried to encourage me to take a leading part in the church. They suggested that they were going to make me a deacon in the church.

I said to them, "I am not old enough to be deacon," but they made me deacon anyhow, even though I was not saved and I didn't know anything about the born again experience. At the same time, outwardly I was a very good person. I did not have any bad habits.

SLOWLY I STARTED DRIFTING AWAY FROM SPIRITUAL THINGS

One day, one younger friend came to me, and he said, "You know, there is a good movie coming," and he gave me the actor's name. I didn't know any actors. I didn't know any of their names because I was not watching any movies, but this boy came in and said, "You're a good singer. You write songs, and you should be learning about more songs and music. Why don't you come to a movie?" I started thinking. I didn't have a radio. We didn't have television at that time. We didn't have any of these things. I thought I would watch movies, learn some songs, and make Christian songs from the music in the movies. I did that and made so many Christian songs from the movie music.

That's the only idea I had, and so I asked my dad, "Dad, can I go and see these movies?"

My dad said, "We are Christian. We are not supposed to go to movies."

I said to my father, "You know I'm a good person. So let me go, and I will not change. I'll be all right. I just want to learn some music so I can put the music in the songs."

So my dad gave me permission, and then I started watching movies. When I saw the first movie, I purchased the movie songbook. I almost memorized all the songs.

I started going to the movies one after another. What happened? Slowly but surely, watching movies changed my life. I started acting like a movie star. I started making my hairstyle like the movie stars, and I started doing dialogue like them and started acting like a movie star. I even wanted to be a movie star.

There was a Christian movie star known to my dad. I said to my dad, "Can you please ask him if he can teach me how to act?"

My father went to him and talked to him, and he said, "Let him finish his college, and we will take him."

I became worse and worse. The change happened slowly, but then I started smoking and drinking. I started going to movies not only one time, but four to five shows every Sunday, going to different theaters.

I had a good job. I had Sundays off and went to church every Sunday. Our pastor used to preach very short sermons, only fifteen to twenty minutes. However, I used to think he was taking a long time, because my mind was not on the service. I was thinking about going and watching the first show at the movie theater. I started feeling guilty. Why was I sitting in the church and thinking about the movies? I tried to shake my head, but the thoughts would not go away. I even tried to choke my neck, but the thoughts would not go away. I started thinking that maybe the thoughts were coming from my heart. I tried to press my heart, but the thoughts would not go away. At the same time, I was thinking, "If this pastor cut short his message, it would be better, because I don't want to miss the first show."

So usually, as soon as the church service finished, I ran to the movies to see the first show. I would never watch the same movie twice. I had to go to different theaters all over Bombay to see different movies. I would watch up to the last show and come home late. My mom would be sitting there and crying, "Son, you're living in Bombay City. There are bad people around there. Somebody will kill you. Why don't you give up watching movies?"

I said, "Mom, nobody has the power to touch me and kill me. I'll be all right."

At the same time, I had some friends who were stronger than me, and so I would go and watch movies with them, so that no one would do harm to me. They were strong boys, and I would go in with them and stand in line for the movies. When there was a new movie with a famous actor, some people would be standing in line at 4 a.m. for the 11 a.m. show. I would go at maybe 10:30 or 10:45 and put some scarf in my neck and one scarf in my hand, showing that I was some macho man. I would put my hand on the shoulder of the man who was first in line, and I would say, "Okay, I'm next. I'll be next." Then I would whistle for the other boys to follow me.

The other people standing in line would say, "Hey, you just came," and I would give them a look as if to say, "Hey, keep your mouth shut, or I'll do something." So everybody would keep quiet. I would go watch that movie, and this is the kind of thing I was doing.

One movie theater had a fence, and only one person could go in at a time. So I stood in line, but as soon as the line started moving, I jumped up and held on the bars that were overhead. I was standing on everybody's head and shoulders and went to the front of the line. They were trying to pull me down, but I was not giving up. They even started tearing my clothes, and that's the way I went to the movies that day.

Why am I saying this? I was addicted to watching movies. Even though I was not doing any other bad things, those movies started ruining my life.

FIRST TIME I HEARD THE SALVATION MESSAGE

One day, one man of God came to our church and started preaching. I wanted him to come and preach in my neighborhood, and so I invited him to my house. After the service he came to my house. I had two houses, and one house had a hall. I said, "We'll gather all my neighbors and have a prayer meeting, and you can preach to these people, because they're all Hindus, Muslims, and all different kinds of people. They should be listening about Jesus Christ."

This man said to me, "The gospel is for you. I want to tell you about Jesus."

I said, "I know everything about Jesus."

He said, "But you have to give your life to Jesus. You have to be born again."

I said, "What do you mean born again?"

He said, "You have to repent of your sins, and you invite Jesus Christ as your Lord and Savior and make Jesus Christ the Lord of your life, and then He will give you grace over sin and you will not sin again."

I said, "This is impossible. There is not a single man in this world that can live without sin. Everybody's a sinner, and every day when I go to bed, I pray, 'Lord, please forgive my sins,' and I go to bed. And the next day I go out and do all kinds of sins, and then I come back and do the prayer, and I believe God hears my prayers."

He said, "That's not the way to do it. The word of God says you should confess your sins and forsake them. Then God will have mercy on you."

I did not listen to this man, but this man kept coming to my house and giving me Bible scriptures. I started listening to everything, but I did not trust that man and what he was saying. This man got so frustrated that he didn't know what to do. He told me later on that he had seen me in a vision when he was in Burma. He did not tell me that, at that particular time, but when he saw me, he did not want to leave my house. He would come regularly and try to teach me the Bible, but there was no change in my life.

FIRST TIME I HEARD THE VOICE OF GOD

It was Easter month, and since I was learning the Bible, I thought that I should read the Bible at the same time that I was going to work. I took my Bible and started reading while I was walking to work, just like people would read the newspaper while they were walking. I was reading about the crucifixion of Jesus Christ.

While I was walking, I heard a voice saying, "You are crucifying Me."

I stopped and looked around. In Bombay City, when you walk in the street, there are hundreds of people walking. When I heard this voice, I thought somebody was saying something. I turned around, but nobody was saying anything to me. So I kept walking.

Again, I heard a voice saying, "You are crucifying Me."

Now at this time, I came to know this has to be God. So I said, "I was not there. Jesus died 2,000 years ago. How can I crucify Him now?"

He said, "I sent the word to you, and you are rejecting My word. You do not pay attention to what My servant is saying. So that means you are crucifying Me again."

I was shocked to hear that, and I started crying. I said, "Lord, please forgive me." I started crying like a baby. My sins started coming in front of my eyes like a movie. I started repenting and said, "Lord, please forgive my sins. Wash me with Your precious blood. Give me victory over these sins in my life. I want to change my life, and I want to be a useful vessel for You." As soon as I prayed this prayer, it was like a burden was lifted away, and I felt some peace in my heart.

I came home after work and said to the man of God, "I received Jesus Christ as my Lord and Savior." I went to my old church where the pastor used to preach fifteen to twenty minutes, and I told everybody, "Come to my house. We have a Bible study." I started going to the neighborhood and bringing people, and we had a Bible study and prayer meeting in my house. I started praying for other people.

Then this man of God took me to a full gospel church, and I took all those people who got saved with me to that church. When I went to that church, I saw that people were praising God, glorifying God, and living clean and holy lives. I started going to that church. I never missed a service -- morning service, evening service, and Bible studies. We used to hold outdoor meetings and preach and tell others about Jesus Christ. I was very much involved in that church. I started praying to God, "Lord, if You call me, I will give up my job and follow You."

WATER BAPTISM

When I learned about baptism, I thought that I had already been baptized, and so I thought that if I took another baptism, the first baptism would be wrong. So I was arguing with people who were talking about water baptism. The Bible says there is only one baptism. That's why I didn't want to take another baptism. However, when I studied carefully, baptism by immersion is the right baptism. When I became convinced in my spirit, I wanted to take the real baptism.

I went to the pastor at the church that I was attending. The pastor was born again, baptized, and filled with the Holy Spirit. I said to that pastor, "Please, baptize me."

He said, "Okay, we do baptisms once a month, and we have to go to the shore. So we are waiting to get more people ready, and then we'll have a baptism service."

I said, "No, sir. You baptize me today, right now."

He said, "Can't you wait until the first of the month?"

I said, "No, if I die right now, what am I going to tell God? When I learned about this, I want to take it right now."

The pastor was very kind and understanding, and he did not

want to disappoint me. He arranged a taxi, and we went to the shore. I was baptized along with two other people, and one of them was my brother. I was very glad that the pastor took special time off and baptized me. I was so grateful to him and God.

The man of God who came to me and taught me about salvation was also teaching about water baptism. I did not like his teaching about water baptism, because he was talking about baptism in Jesus' name only. That's why I did not take water baptism from him. The commandment was given by Jesus Christ to baptize in the name of the Father, Son, and Holy Ghost. I went to a full gospel church and took water baptism from them. Then I tried to convince that man of God that he should be re-baptized. Later on, he was baptized by the same pastor.

Once you know the truth, you should follow the truth, no matter who brings the gospel to you. The word of God is true. In Acts 18, Apollos was a great man. He knew everything about Jesus Christ, but he didn't know anything more about the Holy Spirit. In Acts 19, Paul came to Ephesus and saw Apollos' disciples. He asked them, "Did you receive the Holy Spirit since you believed?" and they said, "We never heard of the Holy Spirit!" Paul re-baptized them. So what I'm trying to say is that even the person who knows about Jesus Christ and the born again experience still might have to learn more about the word of God.

I RECEIVED THE HOLY SPIRIT

When I got saved and baptized, I was so excited. I started studying about the Holy Spirit. The people at the church that I was attending were teaching about the Holy Spirit and encouraging people to receive the Holy Spirit. I learned that the Holy Spirit is very important for doing the Lord's ministry. So I started asking, "Lord, give me the Holy Spirit." The people at the church held a special meeting for people who wanted to receive the Holy Spirit.

I started praying and asking God, "Give me the Holy Spirit," and nothing happened. After several months, I got tired of asking.

One day, someone sent me a letter and wrote, "Brother Peter, we are praying for you. You can ask anything, and God will give it to you, because hundreds of thousands of people are praying for you."

I showed this letter to my younger brother. I said, "What should I ask?"

He said, "Why don't you ask for the Holy Spirit?"

I said, "That's a good idea."

I went to the prayer meeting, and I sat there and prayed, "Lord, this time I'm not going to shout. I'm quietly asking you to give me the Holy Spirit."

At that particular time, I wanted to be a medical doctor. My dad had a friend who was a medical doctor, and I started to go to his clinic and learn more about medicine. I even started getting medicine kits in my house, and if someone had some problem, I used to give them free medicine.

The only reason I wanted to be a medical doctor is that, in my family, most of my brothers and sisters died because they lacked good medical care. For example, one of my brothers had diarrhea, and my father took him to a doctor. The doctor gave my brother an injection in his stomach, and he died. My youngest brother had good eyesight. Nothing was wrong with his eyes; his eyes were just blinking frequently. My dad took him for a check-up. The doctor gave him injections in his eyes, and his eyes popped out like popcorn. He became blind in both eyes.

All of these things I saw. The doctors were charging a lot of money and making a business in India. Most of them didn't care about people; they cared about money. So I thought I would be a medical doctor, and I would give free medicine to people. The burden in my heart was that, even if I became a minister, I would be a medical missionary.

When I was sitting there and praying, asking God to give me

the Holy Spirit, there was another man sitting in front of me. He saw a vision and said to me, "God is showing me something. There is something in your brain, like a knot."

I said, "What?"

He said, "Something is wrong in your mind. It's not a sickness or disease. It's some problem you are having. That's why you are not receiving the Holy Spirit."

I started saying to him, "Wait a minute. I am asking for the Holy Spirit. Why are you getting a vision about me? I want to know directly from God."

I said, "Lord, why are you telling that person what is wrong with me? Why don't you tell me directly?" I asked God, "Lord, tell me, what's wrong with me?"

Then the Lord asked me a question. "Why do you want to be a medical doctor?"

I said to God, "Because in my family, most of my brothers and sisters died from lack of medicine, and I want to be a medical doctor so I can give free medicine." Now, this was not happening so loud. I was speaking in my spirit to God, and God was speaking to me.

I said, "If you give me the Holy Spirit, I will do exactly what Peter, Paul and John did. I will give up the medical practice. I will never go to medical school. I will preach the gospel of Jesus Christ. I will lay hands on the sick, and people will get healed. That's what I want."

As soon as I said this, God filled me with the Holy Spirit, with the evidence of speaking in tongues. I was praising God with another tongue, glorifying God and thanking God. My spirit was lifted up, and I was so happy that God gave me the Holy Spirit. I left the church rejoicing.

The enemy, which is the devil, tried to bring doubt in my mind, telling me that I didn't receive the Holy Spirit, but I had no doubt that I received the Holy Spirit. I was invited to one meeting. I was a little late. Those people were sitting on the floor and praying with their eyes closed. In India, when you go for a prayer meeting in someone's house, you have to take your shoes off outside. I took my shoes off and tiptoed very quietly with my socks, without making any noise. I sat beside someone who was praying, and my elbow touched his elbow. As soon as my elbow touched him, that man started prophesying, "Somebody touched me. That person is filled with the Holy Spirit, and I want to tell you, this person is a man of God."

I had never seen that man before in my life, and he also didn't know me. When he said that, I said, "Thank you, Jesus," and I started praising God. I got assurance that I was filled with the Holy Spirit.

GOD STARTED DOING MIRACLES, AND MY FAITH INCREASED

I was passing by in one neighborhood, and one lady said to me, "Brother Peter, my baby is very sick. She has a very high fever, and she is crying. Could you please pray for her? I know God hears your prayer. You touch her and pray for her."

I just touched that child, rebuked that fever in the name of Jesus, and walked away. While I was walking away, the lady called me back. She said, "My child is healed, no more crying, no more fever." I said, "Thank you, Jesus." This was the first miracle in my life after I received the Holy Spirit.

I knew that God had given me the gift to pray for others. I started going to places to testify and preach. One night, I was on the train coming home from work. It was evening in Bombay, and the train was full. Everyone was reading their newspapers, and there was hardly room to sit. I was standing there and witnessing. I said, "Jesus Christ is a miracle-working God. He is the Savior of the world. He saved me. He delivered me. He did miracles for me."

When I said that, one man said, "If your God is a healer, why are you using eyeglasses?"

Let me tell you why I was using the eyeglasses. You might be saying, "When God healed you in your childhood, what happened?" At that time, I never thought about healing. I never told anybody that Jesus healed my eyes because I was not born again at that time. When I was in school, I could not see anything on the blackboard. I would sit in the first row and look so closely, but still I was not able to see what the teacher was writing. At that time, my father was poor. We didn't have money to go to the eye doctor and get eyeglasses, and so I suffered until I started working. When I finally got eyeglasses, I never thought wearing eyeglasses was wrong. I was using those eyeglasses, and I had no problem until the man questioned me in the train.

I was in a puzzle, but I had faith. I took those eyeglasses, put them in my pocket, put my hand on my eyes, and said, "Lord, give me grace to read what the man is telling me to read." Then I said to this man, "Give me anything to read."

He showed me a newspaper advertisement with very tiny letters. By the grace of God, I was able to read it. When I read it, he started saying, "Those eyeglasses that you are wearing are just for show. You have good eyesight. I don't believe in miracles. I don't believe that this miracle happened right now."

I opened my wallet and showed him the prescription for my eyeglasses, and he stopped arguing with me. I never wore those eyeglasses again, and I praised God for giving me sight.

By the grace of God, God healed me and did miracles in my life, time and time again. When I received the Holy Spirit, I started understanding more about what God can do. The word of God says in Isaiah 53 that "with His stripes, we are healed." Many people do not understand that the healing was done 2,000 years ago on the Cross of Calvary. We have to receive it by faith. Now I was still living my faith life and learning about healings and miracles.

When I was in church, a lady came who was demon-possessed. My pastor was trying to lay hands on her to pray for her, and he was thrown five feet backwards. I saw this with my own eyes. That pastor was a man of God. He told me, "This lady has a demon." However, he could not cast that demon out, and the lady went home.

One day, in the middle of the week, I was just passing by this lady's neighborhood, and she said, "Brother Peter, please come here."

I got really scared. I thought to myself, "This lady has a demon. My pastor could not cast that demon out. Now she is calling me." So I started praying in my heart and asked God to give me grace.

She said, "You know, I went to your church, and that pastor could not cast the demon out." She was telling me how the demon was tormenting her. She said, "Why don't you pray for me?"

I said, "Lord, I believe that You have given me the Holy Spirit. I'm not the healer, You are the healer. You cast this demon out."

I laid hands on her, and she fell flat on her face. Within a few minutes, she stood up and testified, "I feel free. I believe that demon is out of my life."

When I was ordained into the ministry, I was able to baptize her and her husband, daughter, and son-in-law. All glory goes to Jesus Christ.

CALLED FOR THE MINISTRY

When I saw these two miracles, the child who was healed and the demon that was cast out, at that time I was not even a minister. I was just a believer. I started praying, "Lord, now I know you can use me for your glory, but I'm waiting for your calling." I learned that you cannot just give up your job and go preaching the word of God. You have to be called. God has to call you for the ministry. You have to have a definite calling. Otherwise, if you just give up your job and go, the devil will attack you, problems will come, and you will give up the ministry and be in worse condition. I prayed to God, "Lord, please call me, and then I will give up my job."

One day I was in my office. Everybody had a coffee break. It was like 3:00 or 3:30 in the afternoon. Nobody was in my office, and I was in the second floor by myself. I locked the doors, and I was praying.

While I was praying, an angel appeared to me. You may not believe in angels, but I'm telling the truth. If you don't want to believe, it's up to you, but let me tell you what happened. An angel appeared to me as I was in prayer. He had long, black hair, and I saw a paper rolled like a scroll in his hand. He handed the paper over to me. I opened it, and there was a beautiful golden seal. I was attracted to the seal and forgot about reading the paper. As soon as I saw that golden seal, I heard a voice from heaven very clearly.

"I have chosen you for my ministry. If you will not come, I will give your place to somebody."

I shouted, "Lord, I need my place!"

I took that paper and ran to see my brother, who was working in the company next door. I told him what happened. He saw that I was very happy and excited.

I said, "I saw the angel. I heard the voice of God. God is calling me for ministry. You remember we made a promise? If God calls me, I will leave my job and go, and you take care of the family, and if God calls you, you go, and I'll take care of the family?"

He said, "I remember." He was so happy.

I said, "I don't know what happened to the paper. It disappeared from my hand." I went back and forth, looking for the paper, but I could not find it.

My brother said, "Don't worry. I believe it."

I said, "What are you going to do if I give up my job? I am earning more money than you, and you are earning less money than me. If I give up my job, how are you going to feed our family?"

He said, "Brother, you know when Jesus Christ fed the people with the five loaves and two fish, how many people did he feed? More than five thousand. The same God is here. He will take care of our family. You go ahead."

Before I resigned, I went to my pastor and said, "I want to serve the Lord. I want to give up my job."

He said, "Just wait. We are going to have a convention pretty soon. We are having a special meeting, and the chief minister is going to come. He is going to lay hands on people and select them for the ministry. Wait for that day."

I waited. The man came and preached. He said, "How many people want to serve the Lord?" Many people were ready to serve the Lord. He said, "Listen, we are not going to give you any salary. You have to shed your blood, sweat, and tears, and that's what you have to do."

Many people were disappointed and left, but I was sure that I had a calling from God. No one was going to discourage me. I said, "I don't need anything. I am just going to serve the Lord."

The people were waiting there, and this minister said, "This time, I'm going to do a new thing. I'm going to close my eyes, and I'm going to run around and just lay hands on some people. The people on whom I lay hands will be taken for the ministry. The rest of the people will be ordained some other time."

I said in my heart, "Lord, I know you have called me. If this man doesn't lay his hand on me, I will be very disappointed." I prayed and said, "Lord, please tell him to lay his hand on me."

The minister said, "I am closing my eyes. Pastors, please keep your eyes open, because I would not know whom I touched."

The other pastors were watching, and I closed my eyes. The minister started running, and he touched me. Out of many people, less than ten people were chosen, and I was one of them. I was so excited. I started praising and glorifying God. Afterward, all of the pastors who were there laid hands on me and ordained me into the ministry.

I told my boss that I wanted to give up my job and work for the

Lord Jesus Christ. My boss said to me, "Listen, you are so young. Why do you want to give up everything and go? Maybe some European or American people tried to brainwash you. Don't listen to them. You are too young. You can work until you are fifty years old. After fifty years, you can serve the Lord."

I said, "I know you are a religious Hindu. At all of your festivals, you give good fruits to your god. I am young, and I want to serve the Lord in my youth."

He said, "No, please don't do this, because this is Bombay City. Once you lose your job, it will be hard to get a job."

I said, "I'm not looking for a job. I want to serve the Lord."

He said to me, "Find a person just like you, and then I'll release you. Otherwise, I cannot release you."

I said, "Where am I going to find a person like me? There is one brother like me next door. I can tell him to come and take this job."

When I came home from work, I said to my father, "Dad, I want to go and preach the gospel."

He said, "Where are you going?"

I said, "I'm going to leave Bombay, go around the world, and preach the gospel."

My father said, "No, no. You are a firstborn son. You have the responsibility to take care of the family. Stay in Bombay City. There are millions of people here. Preach the gospel to them. You don't have to give up Bombay City and go somewhere else."

I said to my father, "Do you know what Jesus said? He said to forsake all and follow him. I want to forsake all and follow the Lord. Dad, you are a minister. The word of God says that you should dedicate your first son to the Lord."

He said, "Okay, I give you to the Lord."

Then I talked to my mother. She started crying. I said, "Mom, why are you crying?"

She said, "I'm not going to let you go." She held my hand and started crying. "I don't want you to go. You can stay here and serve the Lord."

I said, "Mom, let me ask you a question. Four of your sons and two of your daughters died. What did you do? You could not do anything. If I disobey God and die tonight, what are you going to do?"

She said, "I cannot do anything."

I said, "Then let me go. If I go, God will bless you, and I'll try to help the family."

My mother said, "Okay, son, you go and serve the Lord."

That's the way I started my journey. By the grace of God, God is so faithful to me. He supplied all my needs. Philippians 4:19 says, "My God will supply all your needs according to His riches in glory by Christ Jesus," and that word is true. That Scripture is true in my life.

I believe that God can do the same for you. If you are not saved, and you have any problems, I have good news for you. Jesus Christ loves you. Jesus Christ came from heaven and died on the cross of Calvary, just for you. When I received Jesus Christ as my Lord and Savior, He changed my life.

The same Jesus wants to change you. Just simply say, "Jesus, come into my life. Be my Lord. Be my Savior. I commit my life into Your loving hands. Forgive all my sins. Wash me with Your precious blood. Touch me, and heal me." He will do it. Once you receive Jesus Christ as your Lord and Savior, you will never be the same. You will be completely transformed, and you will be a living witness to others.

two

✿

MY FAITH MINISTRY STARTED

At this time, I was spiritually growing, learning more about God, and my faith was getting stronger in the Lord.

JOURNEY OF FAITH

I left home with my shirt and pants and nothing else. We had one Bible that was a family Bible, and so I did not even take a Bible with me, because I wanted that Bible for the family. That's the way I left my home.

The church that I was attending had special Bible classes for people who were ordained for the ministry. We used to get up early in the morning, and we would be praying from 4:00 to 9:00. After that, we would have breakfast, and then we would have Bible classes until 1:00. After that, we would have our lunch, and then we would go out to visit church members and have meetings in their houses. We would come home at maybe 9:00 or 10:00. We would have our dinner and then an hour of night prayer, and then we would go to bed. That was our routine every day.

I was very happy serving the Lord, and I knew that God was

with me. I was following Jesus Christ, and I knew in my heart that He had called me definitely. The man who was in charge at the church saw God's hand in my life, and he started taking me on trips to conventions in different parts of India to pray for sick people. I was given a chance to preach in a big church for the first time. There were some other ministers working and studying with me, and some of them were a little bit jealous. They started saying, "This is a newcomer, why are you giving this man a chance? We have been here for ten years, why are you not giving us a chance to preach in this big church?" I could see the jealousy among the brethren, but I didn't care, because I was following the Lord.

One day, the pastor of the church said, "There is a need for a pastor in one church. Will you go?"

I said, "Yes, I will," but then I started thinking, "I'm too young to go right now and take care of a big church." I was reading the Bible, and the word of God came to me from the book of Jeremiah: "Do not say, 'I am a youth,' for you shall go to all to whom I send you, and whatever I command you, you shall speak.'" When the word of God came to me, I was bold enough to go.

By the grace of God, I went there and preached the word. I was so busy. I used to conduct morning and evening services, as well as midweek Bible studies, outdoor meetings, and meetings in believers' houses. We were growing, and there was no room in that church. I talked to the believers and said, "We need a bigger hall." They agreed, and we got a bigger place.

Then the pastor transferred me to another church. The pastor there was so proud that English was his primary language, and he started giving me a hard time for no reason. I didn't mind because I was still studying and learning the word of God. I thought that, being his assistant, I would learn something from him, but I could not learn anything from him, because he was struggling himself to get a message from the Lord to preach every Sunday.

One day, he asked me, "Would you take the Sunday service today?"

I said, "Okay," and I started preaching every Sunday. I asked him, "Why are you asking me to preach every Sunday? You are the pastor."

He said, "I pray and pray, but I don't get the right subject to preach, but you have a message all the time."

I said, "Sir, it's because I'm called by God."

I would preach for half an hour, and he would get some inspiration to elaborate on what I said.

Then he asked me to go to different houses and conduct Bible studies there. Our church had other branches, and he asked me to conduct Bible studies there as well. By the grace of God, I learned the Bible very well. However, even though I was helping this pastor in various ways, he was still giving me a hard time.

I was wearing shoes, and he said, "You're wearing shoes, and I'm wearing sandals. You should not be wearing shoes, because I am the pastor here, and you are the assistant here. You should take off your shoes." However, he did not give me sandals. He said, "We will order you sandals," but he did not let me use my shoes in the meantime. I took my shoes off, and, as you know, if you don't have practice, walking on mountain roads without shoes will be difficult. I had a hard time walking without sandals.

I was thinking, "Why is this man allowing me to suffer like this without a cause?" However, I thought this might be one of my trainings, and so I did not complain to anyone.

One day, the people from the water department came to shut off the water. I was taking a shower at the time. I had just begun using the soap when the pastor came knocking on the shower door and told me to come out and talk to them, because he didn't know their language. I told him that I wanted to finish my shower, but he said that I had to come out and talk to them right away, and that they would shut off the water otherwise. I came out of the shower still covered in soap and talked to them.

They told me, "We gave this man six months' notice to check

the meter, and he did not do anything. That's why we are shutting off the water."

I said, "Can you give me twenty-four hours more? Tomorrow at this time, the meter will be fixed. If the meter is not fixed, then you can shut off the water."

Although they could not believe that I could fix it within twenty-four hours, they did not turn off the water that day, and I finished my shower.

After they left, the pastor was angry at me and said, "I could not fix it within six months. How are you going to fix it within twenty-four hours? You should have asked for more time."

I said, "Sir, God is able to do it. God doesn't need twenty-four hours. He can do it before that."

We took the meter to a mechanic. He was not able to open it and began to bang it with a hammer.

I told him, "Don't bang it. You will break the glass."

He became angry and said, "Take this meter somewhere else. I cannot do it."

The pastor was angry with me and said, "Where are we going to find another mechanic in this town?"

I said, "Don't worry. We will take it directly to the water supply company, where they test the meters."

We went to the water supply company to test the meter. The man who was testing the meters said to me, "In order for your meter to pass the test, we have to let one thousand gallons of water go through your meter. If your meter is over by ten gallons, then it fails. Then you have to purchase another meter."

I laid my hand on the meter and prayed, and he took the meter for testing. When he was testing five hundred gallons of water, the meter showed 505 gallons. He came to me and said, "Your meter has failed. It is already 505 gallons, and if I put five hundred more, it will be 1,010 gallons."

I said, "Please test five hundred more gallons, and the meter will adjust and will not go over." As we did the testing, the meter passed, by the grace of God.

Even though the meter passed, we had to sign some papers and certify the meter, and the person who was in charge was not there. They said that the forms were in his office, and that he would be back the following day.

I said, "Lord, tomorrow those people are coming to shut off the water. What am I going to do?" I just walked around, and I found a form on the floor.

I took that form, and I came back and said, "Is this the form?"

He said, "Yes, where did you get it?"

I said, "I got it from the floor in that other building."

He said, "Okay, that's the form. I'm going to sign it." He certified it, and we got the meter.

The following day, we showed the certification to the people from the water department. The pastor was very happy that we were able to get everything done within twenty-four hours. From that day onward, he had a lot of great respect for me and did not give me a hard time there anymore.

Another pastor came to me and said, "There is a state called Gujarat. In that state, it's really hard to win souls. We have been struggling there for ten to twelve years, and no souls have been added to the church. Could you please come and take over?"

I prayed and said, "Lord, if you want me to go there and start your work, give me grace."

The central pastor, who was in charge of Bombay, gave me the key to the building, as well as directions to get there. I started my journey in the evening by train. While I was going, I lost the address of the building. When I reached Gujarat in the morning, I came out of the train, and there were several horse buggies and taxi drivers. I preferred to take a horse buggy, and the driver asked me where I wanted to go.

I said, "I lost the address, but I remember one thing. The

address said something about a circle. Do you know anything about a circle?"

He said, "I'll take you there."

We went to the circle, and in that circle, there were seven roads. He said, "Which way do you want to go?"

I said, "I don't know because I lost the address. We'll take each road, one by one, and we will find the street."

He said, "Do you know these streets? It's, like, fifteen to twenty-five miles. When we go there and come back, we won't be able to go another day."

I said, "However many days it takes, I will pay for you, but we are going to find it."

We took the main road, and I stopped at a barber shop. I asked the barber, "Did you see anybody going with a Bible in their hand, walking in this street anytime?"

He said, "Yes, on Sunday."

I thought to myself, "This is it." I told the driver to turn here, and then we came to the building. I recognized the building, because I had seen it in a dream earlier. I opened the door with the key.

It was nighttime, and I was very tired and fell asleep. There was a knock at the door. I opened the door, and a man asked me, "Are you Brother Peter? We went to the railway station to look for you. My mother cooked food for you. Could you please come for dinner?"

I was hungry, and so I went with him and had a wonderful dinner. I thank God for how He took care of me that day.

FIRST SERVICE IN THAT TOWN

No one showed up for my first service, except for one Hindu man.

I asked him, "Do you know anything about Jesus Christ?"

He said, "I know everything about Jesus Christ and Christianity."

I asked him, "Do you know the Bible?"

He said, "I know the Bible very well."

I knew that he was not telling the truth, and so I gave him some chapters from the book of Revelation and asked him to explain them to me. Instead of admitting that he did not understand, he just started to say whatever came to mind, and he did not make any sense. Then he changed the subject and asked me a question.

"Are you new here?"

I said, "Yes, I'm new here. I don't know the language or the people here."

He said, "I will introduce you to a Hindu group. They will give you food, money, and whatever you need."

I said, "Sir, I did not come here begging for bread. I came here to preach the gospel of Jesus Christ. Let me tell you, the day will come that you will be lying helpless on your bed, and no Hindu people will help you. At that time, God will give me grace to help you. Remember this."

Within a few months, this man sent some Christian brother to tell me that he was lying in bed with severe pain. He said, "Please come and help me."

I went to the house where he was, and I asked what happened to him. He told me that his friend came to wake him up for construction work and threw an axe at him, which hit him in the knee, and he had much pain and swelling. His friend left him, and no Hindu people gave him anything. By the grace of God, I was able to give him some food and money.

I said to him, "Do you remember what I said, on the first Sunday that you came to our church? Where are your Hindu friends?"

He said, "When you are in trouble, nobody helps."

I laid hands on him, prayed for him, and invited him to come to church. He came to church and never talked about his religion again.

By the grace of God, I was able to visit different neighborhoods. Slowly but surely, people started coming to church, and some of the people were ready for water baptism. I wrote to our ministry headquarters that someone should come to baptize these people, because I was very young. (In that church, they would not allow ministers to perform baptisms unless they were in the ministry for at least fifteen years.) The central pastor sent someone to baptize the people, but after he left, there were more people who were ready for baptism. I wrote to them again to send someone to help me, and the central pastor, who had baptized me, gave me authority to baptize people, because I was far away and it would have been difficult for them to send ministers all the time. I was so happy and started praising and thanking God for giving me the opportunity to baptize people without anyone's help.

I stayed in that state for at least eight years. I learned the language and preached the gospel there. Many people were saved and baptized. Many miracles happened, and God did a great work in that city. Whatever we needed for the ministry, God gave it to me.

three

✿

FIRST OPEN MEETING IN THAT TOWN

When I arrived at the circle with the seven roads, I thought that I would like to hold an open air meeting.

THEY WANTED TO CHANGE MY PLAN

There was a city playground very close to my church. I went to the person who was in charge of that playground and took permission to have healing services for ten days. I started fasting and praying for this special meeting. I told other people about the meeting, and we were very excited about it. I rented a tent and put up a stage. I called an electrician and put lights everywhere. I called people who had loudspeaker sets and put four speakers on the roof of the playground office, pointing in four directions, north, south, east, and west. My voice could be heard from five to seven miles away. The meeting was ready to go.

On the first day, the meeting started at maybe 8:00 in the evening, and many people gathered. After the meeting, I gave an altar call. I said that if anyone was sick, I could pray for them.

The first person who came for prayer had a problem with his eye. After I prayed for him, his eye was completely normal. He gave his testimony, and many people were lined up for prayer. The blind and the crippled were healed, and many miracles happened. The meeting closed at 11:00 at night, and many policemen were surrounding the playground and asking if the miracles really happened or if people were faking.

The person who was in charge of the playground was a little bit scared and wanted to close the meeting because Hindu people were coming there. He thought that Christianity was spreading, and he didn't want to give me nine more days. He said, "This ground is too small, so you should have a bigger ground. I'll give you a bigger ground. Stop these services."

I knew in my heart that he was lying and that he just wanted to shut down the services.

Then he said, "Come to my house, and we will discuss this."

I was suspicious, but I told my church members to pray for me. As soon as the meeting was over, almost at midnight, I went to his house. Almost a dozen city government officials were there. They told me that I should not hold my meeting at the playground because it was too small. They also said, "The people might hurt you, so we are trying to save your life."

I said, "I'm not hurting anyone. I'm helping people. People are being healed. So I don't think any of them want to hurt me. Even if someone kills me, I'm not afraid of dying. If you want, I can write down on paper that you're not responsible. I'm doing this at my own risk." I asked them a question. "Are you against Christianity?"

They said, "No." There was religious freedom, and so they couldn't say anything. They could not stop me, and so they said okay.

I continued for the full ten days. I told the people who provided the tent, the electrical equipment, and the loudspeakers,

"Please take everything away on the tenth day. Afterward, I'm not responsible."

When the meeting was finished, I praised the Lord for the success of our services. Nobody was killed or injured, but God healed so many people. After midnight, there was heavy wind and rain. The tent was flattened, and everything was in disarray.

The next morning, the same man who had told me not to hold the meeting came and thanked me. He said, "I'm sorry that I told you not to have services for ten days. For ten days, there was no problem. After the service, when this heavy rain came, I came to know that God is really with you. He gave you great success, and only after the meeting was this great disaster. I'm sorry that I disturbed you."

MOVING TO A BETTER PLACE

I said to our church landlord, "There is enough room on the plot where our church is. Can you build a bigger hall for me?" I told him, "The time will come when the people will be sitting in front of the church and across the street."

He said, "I would like to see that day."

I had special meetings for Good Friday and Easter. I went to the city and took a permit to put loudspeakers on top of our church building. Instead of taking a permit for three days, I took a permit for a year. In the middle of our service, one man came to me and said, "Do you have a license to use loudspeakers?"

I said, "Please don't disturb the service. I'll come outside and talk to you." I told him, "I don't have to turn off the loudspeakers, because I have a permit. If I want to, I can have a service every day." When I showed him that I had a permit for the whole year, God shut his mouth and he never bothered me again.

When I had the meeting with the loudspeaker, people were

sitting outside the building and standing across the street, and so God fulfilled what I said.

After that, I started praying for a new building.

There was one Hindu contractor who used to come to our church. He believed Jesus Christ, and he used to pray to Jesus Christ for his business. God gave him much success. He even named his grandson Jesus, in the Gujarati language. He had a great respect for me.

One day, I thought I would go and ask him if he had any building for rent. He was taking a nap under a tree. I just stood there and didn't bother to wake him up, but he heard my steps. He looked at me and said, "What can I do for you?"

I asked him if there was any building for rent.

He said, "I just finished constructing a building, but the electrical wiring still has to be done."

I said, "How much will be the rent?"

He said, "Before you, two people came asking for this building. One was asking two hundred fifty, one was asking three hundred. But I rejected their offers."

"This is not for me, I'm sorry," I said. I just wanted to walk away.

He said, "How much can you afford? Tell me."

I said, "I can afford only fifty."

Then he said, "Okay, you can have it. It's yours."

I said, "Why didn't you give it to them for a higher price, and you're giving it to me for fifty?"

He said, "I was lying down, and I saw a dream that you were coming and asking for the building. Even if you had offered a dollar, I would have given it to you for a dollar."

He continued, "But there is a problem that I have. In the same plot, there is another tenant, and he fights with me all the time. I cannot even go and collect the rent from him. How are you going to handle that person?" That person was a businessman with a silk factory, where he used to keep silkworms to make the silk.

I said, "If God gives me the building, God will give me the grace to conduct services there without a problem." Then I said, "Don't worry. I'll call the electrician and do the wiring and everything. You just do the paperwork."

He said, "No, I will do everything for you."

The contractor did all the electricity and painting, and the building was ready to use.

Before the first services started, I was washing the front porch with soap and water. The rich neighbor, who had the silk business, came and said, "You are a man of God. You are not supposed to do this kind of washing and cleaning. I will do it for you." He had several grown children, but he did not ask them to help me. Instead, he himself started cleaning in front of our church. The contractor, who was my new landlord, came and saw that the silk factory owner was cleaning our front yard, and he was surprised.

I invited this neighbor to come and attend the service. He came and sat in the church, and then the contractor came and sat beside him. After the service, I shook both of their hands, and I told them to shake each other's hands. They did, and from that day forward, they had no dispute with each other and were friendly.

This place was surrounded by Hindu residences. All of my neighbors were Hindu, but by the grace of God, Hindus and Christians were coming and worshipping together. This was the last building that I had in Gujarat, before God called me to come to America.

LARGEST TOWN MEETING IN GUJARAT

After our successful meeting on the city playground, I was thinking about renting a hall instead, so that we would not have any problems from the public. I started praying about it. There was a big town hall in the middle of the city. That was the largest town hall in Gujarat. One of our church members suggested that we should have a meeting there. I was told that no missionaries had used that hall for Christian services.

I went to the town hall office to find out how I could rent the place. When they asked me for what purpose I would use the hall, I said that I wanted to preach the gospel and heal the sick.

They said, "Apply ten days in advance, and you will get it."

I was a little suspicious that they might not give it to me in ten days, and so I applied a year in advance. That gave me a chance to prepare, advertising in newspapers and making large billboards. We even took a painting crew and painted on the highway. We printed so many flyers in English as well as the local language, and I sent them to different states too. Although we were excited about the meeting, I waited for a whole year, and no one replied that our application was renewed.

With only one day remaining before the meeting, I wanted to talk to the people at the town hall office and ask them why they did not give me approval. The office was a couple of miles away, and I decided to walk there.

It was a hot, sunny day, and I was sweating. I started thinking in my head, "Lord, if you could put one drum of water on the street, I would be so happy, and I would cool myself." While I was walking, I saw that, on the side of the street, there was a metal drum filled with water. I thought that the water might be warm, because it was a hot day. It was filled to the rim, so that I didn't have to bend down to use it. I looked around to see if someone had kept the water there, if there was any construction work going on, but I didn't see anyone in that place. I thought in my heart, "I don't care who says what, God answered my prayer." I thanked God, and I washed my head with that water and felt cool and refreshed.

However, I started looking in my pocket for a comb, because I had messed up my hair. Then I said, "Lord, I'm going to go to the office, and I cannot go with messed-up hair. I'll have to go back home." I looked at the ground, and there was a small comb in a small, plastic package. I picked up the comb, to see the name of the company on it, and the word "Amen" was written on it. I thanked God for answering my prayer. I opened the seal of the brand new comb, combed my hair, and went to the office.

After arriving at the office, I talked to a clerk. He said, "Sir, you have to apply ten days in advance." I showed him my application. The date of the application was one year in advance, with only one day remaining.

He said, "Wait a minute," and he went inside. He came back and said, "Sorry, the person who approves applications isn't here."

"Is there anyone who can approve it? Tomorrow is going to be my healing service," I said. "I advertised everywhere, and if you don't give it to me today, I'm going to put a tent in front of the town hall. Otherwise, you have to give me a letter saying that you are not giving your hall for Christian programs. If you give me the letter, then I will call the higher government authorities and find out why you did not give it to me."

As soon as I said that, he said, "Wait a minute." He went inside and talked to somebody. Then he came back and said, "How many days do you want?"

I said, "One day."

Then he said, "We are approving your application, not only for one day, but for ten days."

I was not planning for ten days, but he was offering it. I said, "I'll take it."

He said, "We will not only give it to you for ten days, but we will also give you a cleaning crew. You won't have to worry about anything."

I was so happy. I started praising and glorifying God, and I gave the good news to the church members. By the grace of God, we started our first service in that hall. The blind and deaf were healed, and many miracles happened. People came from out of town for the services. The meeting was successful, and it did not cost me a dime. Everything was free.

After that, there were some people ready for water baptism.

We didn't have any transportation to take them for baptism, and we would have to travel more than twenty miles. We decided to charter a bus. We took some tambourines and went with singing and rejoicing.

The manager of that transportation company said, "Can I come with you to see your baptism service?"

I was a little bit hesitant, because he was Hindu. I thought he might make some trouble. I said to him, "It's your bus. You don't have to ask our permission."

We baptized people at the harbor, where there was enough water. We held the baptism service successfully, without anybody disturbing us. We returned, rejoicing, to the bus terminal. As the other believers were going home, I went to the manager's office. I asked him how much I had to pay for chartering the bus.

He said, "Zero."

I thought he was kidding. I told him, "You have to tell me really how much."

He said, "No, you did a great service to the city. I really enjoyed the trip with you, and you don't have to pay anything."

So I thanked God, that He made the impossible things possible for us. That was my first special revival meeting in that town hall. Once I got the biggest town hall in the state, I had no problem getting other town halls in other places.

SPECIAL MEETING IN HINDU AND MUSLIM TOWN

One day, an evangelist came to me and said, "Let's do some evangelical work in my town."

We went walking around town, looking for a place, and in the middle of the city, I found some open ground with a fence around it. I said to this brother, "This place looks good for a one day meeting."

He said, "We cannot have a meeting here, because on this ground, all the merchants come and hold their bazaars. So I don't think they will be giving it to us."

I said, "Do they do it on Saturday?"

He said, "Saturday, it might be open."

So I said, "Take me to the place where we can get a permit."

I went to the police station, talked to the chief police officer, and said, "I would like to have a meeting tomorrow on the ground where they do the bazaar."

He said, "What are you going to do there?"

I said, "Gospel addresses and divine healing services." I don't know if he understood or not. He asked me twice, and I gave him the same answer twice.

He said, "I will give you permission, and no one will bother you. "

I said, "Could you tell some of the officers in front of me, so that they will not come and stop the service?"

So he called a couple of officers and introduced them to me. I knew that now they would not bother me, and they might even help me while I was conducting the service. I was so thankful to God that, within a short period of time, God gave me grace to have a permit.

I had only sixty-seven Indian pennies in my pocket, but I didn't tell anyone. I rented certain things that I needed, such as a stage and portable lights. Then I asked one of the nearby merchants if I could pull some electrical lights from his shop, to bring some light to the stage, as his shop was adjacent to the bazaar ground. Everything was ready to go, and the meeting was set for the evening.

There was a church a couple of miles away from that area. I went to that church and talked to the pastor. I asked him, "Can your people come and sing at this meeting?"

He said, "No, I cannot send anybody there to sing. There are Muslims living in that area, and they might cause some problem."

I left that place, and as I was walking on the street, I saw a beggar sitting on the roadside. I looked at him, and he was completely blind. God inspired me to pray for him.

When I went close to him, he said to me, "Son, whatever you are giving me, put it in this jar."

I said to the man, "I'm going to pray for you, and God is going to open your blind eyes. I'm going to pray for you in the name of Jesus."

He said, "I don't believe in Jesus. I believe in Him as a prophet, not as God."

"Jesus opened my eyes, and I am able to see. The same Jesus is able to open your eyes," I said. "I'll give you five minutes to make a decision, whether or not I should pray for you. When you decide, just raise your hand."

I started praying in my heart. I said, "Lord, let him raise his hand so that I can pray for him. I believe in my heart that you're going to heal him."

All of a sudden, he raised his hand.

I put my thumbs on his eyes and said, "In the name of Jesus, be healed." I took my hands off of his eyes and said to him, "Open your eyes and see."

He said, "I can see! I can see cars! I can see people! I can see everything!"

I started thinking in my heart, "If I tell this story to anyone, no one is going to believe it."

However, there was a man standing maybe ten feet away, and he was watching while I was praying for the blind man. He came and said to me, "I was Hindu. I became Christian. I read in the Bible that Jesus did so many miracles, but this is the first miracle that I saw with my own eyes." He started thanking God.

The blind man got up and started walking. I told him, "Tonight we will have a prayer meeting for sick people. Please go and tell someone what Jesus has done for you, and tell people to come to the meeting."

I was so happy. I came back and told the evangelical brother who was living in that town. I was a guest in the house where he was living with his sister, who was a medical doctor. "I believe many people will come for the meeting," I told him. "We will need some volunteers to control the crowd."

As I didn't have any money in my pocket, except for sixty-seven Indian pennies, I wasn't able to do any advertisement -- no flyers, no radio ads, no billboards, nothing. I depended on word of mouth, and I believed that God would bring the souls. We had one blind man's witness, as well as the other man who was also a witness to me that he saw the blind man being healed. I also told the church people to come.

By the grace of God, in the evening, the ground was almost completely filled with people. On the stage, I started with prayer and singing, but the people were not interested in listening to songs. They thought that this might be some kind of fundraising propaganda, and they wanted to go away. I told the people, "Please don't go away. I'm going to stop my singing. I'm going to pray for you and your needs. When I tell you to leave, you won't want to go. You will be rushing toward the healing lines." We made two lanes, one for ladies and one for men.

When I started preaching, people were quietly listening to the word of God. When I finished my preaching, I gave the altar call for healing. One man came running and jumped on the platform where I was standing. God gave me courage to ask him, "What can I do for you?"

He said, "I would like to tell you what happened to me. I was listening to your preaching about Jesus Christ, and God did a miracle for me. In my ear, it was as if someone was beating a drum for thirteen years, and I never had peace. But when I heard the word of God, that noise completely stopped. I don't want that noise coming back to my ears, so please pray."

I encouraged the people. "If God can heal this person without anyone touching him -- the word of God healed him -- the same God can heal you today."

People started coming and lining up. They were pushing each other and giving a hard time to the volunteers. So the volunteers started saying, "Brother Peter, please stop this healing service because we are being crushed."

I told the audience, "Please don't push anyone. I will be praying for everyone. I will not be leaving the stage until I have prayed for everyone." After that, nobody pushed anyone, and I prayed for everyone. God healed so many people.

After the service, some people shook my hand and put money in my hand. I went to the people from whom I rented the stage, portable lights, and electrical equipment. I wanted to pay them for their services, because I now had money to pay them. Nobody took my money, however. They said, "We saw that you were a help to our town, so we don't want to charge you anything."

Then I went to the house where I was staying with that evangelical brother. We prayed a prayer of thanksgiving, and I went to bed. At about 1:00 in the morning, we heard a knock on the door. That brother went to answer the door, and there were so many people standing outside. They said, "Bring that minister down, so that he can pray for us."

This brother told them, "He is very tired, he is sleeping. But if you need prayer, he is going to one village. I'll give you the address, and you can go there."

The next day, we went to that village, and we had three days of meetings in that village. The meetings were arranged by a brother who had a tailoring business in the village with his wife. By the grace of God, this village was conveniently located near a government bus terminal, so that people from the other towns also came to these meetings.

I was praying at the postmaster's house that God should do miracles in these three days of meetings, when a young Hindu man came to the house and asked if I could pray for him.

I said, "What kind of problem do you have?"

He said, "I have throat cancer."

I said, "Tonight we're going to have a meeting in one village. Please come, so that I can pray for you there."

He said, "Why can't you pray for me here?"

I said, "When you come there, you will see other people get healed, and your faith will be increased."

He said, "I am a sick man. I am tired. I cannot come there. Please pray for me, and I have enough faith that God will heal me."

I said, "I pray for people in Jesus' name. If you believe Jesus can heal you, I can pray for you."

I touched his throat and prayed in the name of Jesus. After praying, I asked him, "How do you feel?"

He said, "I don't feel any pain."

I gave him a glass of water, at least sixteen ounces. I prayed over the water and said, "Please drink this."

He said, "I could not eat or drink anything, because it gives me a lot of pain, and I could not swallow anything."

I said, "Sir, I prayed for you. Jesus healed you. When you drink this, you will know that you are healed."

He drank the whole glass, and he didn't have any pain.

I said to him, "Jesus already healed you. Go home and eat the best dinner, and tell someone what Jesus Christ has done."

That evening, we started our first healing service, and I testified about that man. I prayed for the people who came from out of town, and the three days of meetings were so successful, that I cannot tell you everything in detail.

I had rented a taxi for three days, and after the third day, I went to return it to the man from whom I had borrowed it. He was also a Hindu man, and he had several taxis.

I asked him, "Could you tell me how much I have to pay for three days?"

He said, "You don't have to pay anything."

I started thinking that he might be kidding.

He said, "No, I'm serious. I'll tell you why I'm not charging you. Three days ago, I sent my brother-in-law to see you for prayer. He had throat cancer. You prayed for him, and since then he has no pain. He is eating well and has no trace of cancer. He spent thousands of dollars paying for medicine and doctors' fees. Instead of getting better, he was getting worse. I thank God that, by your prayer, my brother-in-law is healed. So I cannot take any money from you."

I said, "God bless you. Go and tell others what God has done for you."

I thank God for what God did. I started thanking God that all my needs were met. I told you earlier that I only had sixty-seven Indian pennies in my pocket. In today's currency, that is one American penny. God helped me time and time again. Our God is an all-sufficient God. Philippians 4:19 says, "But my God shall supply all your need according to His riches in glory by Christ Jesus."

four

✿

THE LORD'S MINISTRY STARTED GROWING

I used to take my bicycle and visit people in different neighborhoods to talk about Jesus Christ. One day, one man saw me and invited me to his house. He took me into a really dark room, and I said, "What are you going to do?"

He said, "I'm going to kill you."

I said, "What did I do?"

He said, "You're preaching about Jesus Christ. We are not Christian here. We do not want to know anything about Jesus."

I said, "Sir, you have no power to kill me. Nobody is there to save me, but my God is greater than your god."

He said, "I'm going to make you vomit blood, and you're going to die here."

I said, "Okay. Try everything."

He could not make me vomit blood.

"Okay, give me a few minutes. Let me pray first, and then you can kill me," I said. "Is there anyone sick in your family?"

He said, "My wife is in the hospital. She is dying."

I said, "Well, you're going to kill me. If you let me go, I'll go and pray for your wife."

He said, "Go and pray for her."

I said, "Okay." I did not promise to come back. I just said, "Okay, I'll go and pray for your wife." I went and prayed for his wife, and his wife was healed. She came home, and she told him what happened.

Later, I was walking along the same street as that man's house. As I passed by his front door, he bowed down and started saluting me.

"Are you going to kill me?" I said.

"No," he said. "God heard your prayer, and my wife is completely healed.

One day, one of my church members and I were going to pray for one of his co-workers, who was sick. While we were going, we saw a group of people camping in the street and raising funds to build a Hindu temple. There was a Hindu priest standing on one leg for eighteen years. Many people were standing there and listening to this man's message.

As I was standing there and watching, one man came to me and said, "You look like a salesperson. You might have some money in your bag. Could you give us at least ten dollars?"

I said, "Before I can do anything, I want to say something."

This man whispered to that Hindu priest who was standing on one leg, and he got permission for me to say something.

I took my Bible and read from Acts 7:48 that God does not live in a handmade temple. 1 Corinthians 3:16 says that we are the temple of the living God. We have to invite Jesus Christ into our hearts. He will come and dwell in this temple, and our lives will be changed. I preached the word of God there for a couple of hours, and they were not able to stop me.

I looked at my watch, and I said, "Sir, I have to go because we have another appointment. I'll be back."

The Hindu priest was very angry because I was a young man

preaching about Jesus Christ in front of him and all of the other people there who were Hindu. He said, "You have your mother's milk on your lips, and you are teaching us? I want to see if your God is so powerful."

The Hindu priest went behind me, took a jar of water, and put some powder in it. I didn't know what he was doing, but the church member who came with me was watching.

He said to me in a different language, "Please don't drink that water, because that man put some powder in it."

I said to him, "Please don't say anything. Just pray for me. God will do a miracle."

The Hindu priest gave me that jar and said, "Drink this."

I said to him, "I'm not thirsty."

He said, "If you don't drink, I won't let you go."

Mark 16:18 says that if you drink any deadly, poisonous thing, it will not harm you. I said, "Lord, I trust in your word. I did not want to drink. I told him I'm not thirsty, but he is forcing me to drink this. Otherwise, they are going to kill us." I laid my hand on the jar and prayed, "Lord, sanctify this, whatever it is. I am going to drink it in your name." I said that and took the jar, believing that there was no poison in it and that God took care of it. I drank the jar and gave the empty jar back to the Hindu priest.

I said, "Is that okay with you now?"

He said, "Now you can go."

I said, "I'll be back because I have an appointment with another person. After that, I'll come back."

They had been camping there for six months, and they were not planning to leave until they had reached their fundraising goal. However, when I came back, nobody was there. They left because they thought that I was going to die.

There was a hospital within walking distance, and the church member who was with me advised me, "Let's go to the hospital and take the poison out. I don't want you to die like that."

I said, "I prayed over it, and I didn't die up to now. Even if I go to the hospital, if I'm supposed to die, the doctor has no power to keep me alive."

I did not go to the hospital. I went home and praised and glorified God. This happened a long time ago, and I'm still alive. Our God is a good God. He is a miracle-working God.

PREACHING IN THE MUSLIM MOSQUE

One day, a Muslim priest came to our church while I was out of town. He knew that we were doing healing services in our church, and many people were coming and getting healed. We never charged anyone a penny, but this man was telling people to bring coconuts, sugar, flowers, and things like that to his mosque. So, his business was going down, as people started coming to our church for healing.

This Muslim priest told one of our church members, "When your pastor comes, send him to my mosque."

The church member said, "Why do you want him to be there?"

The Muslim priest said, "Oh, we want to know more about Jesus," but he was lying. He wanted to kill me.

I said to our church member, "We don't have to go there. They don't want to believe Jesus Christ. They just want to harm us."

He said, "I promised that man that I will make an appointment for you, and my pastor will be there. So, they will be waiting for us."

I went with a few church members, and when we arrived, the Muslim priest was already preaching in his mosque against Christianity and blaspheming Christ in front of us.

I said to the church member who arranged the meeting, "Can you hear what this man is saying? Do you think this man who is talking bad about our Christianity wants to hear about Jesus?"

So he said, "If you don't want to preach, let's go."

I said, "No, I'm going to preach the Word."

I started praying, and then the Muslim priest came to me and said, "Would you like to preach now?"

I said to him, "Tell the audience that you invited me to preach in your mosque. Tell them that I am a servant of the Lord Jesus Christ."

After he introduced me properly, I stood there and preached the word of God.

I said, "Jesus Christ came into this world. He died for you. He took your sickness and disease. Jesus said, 'Freely ye have received, freely give' (Matthew 10:8). It's not good to charge anything for prayer." I asked the audience, "How many years have you been coming to the mosque?"

Some said that they had been coming for two years, three years, or five years.

I said, "Did any of you get healed?"

They said, "No," but they kept on coming and giving coconuts, sugar, and oil.

I said, "If anyone comes to our church, we do not charge them anything."

I was going to give out cards with my church address on them and invite people to come to our church. In the meantime, my church member said to me, "These people don't want our cards. They want to kill us."

I said to him, "You and all the church members go out."

He said, "What about you?"

I said, "I'll be here. God will protect me."

After I finished preaching, I said, "It's too late at night now. I'll come back some other time."

However, those people surrounded me with knives and rods in their hands. They said, "We are not going to let you go. We are going to kill you."

I wanted to get out of that place. In a mosque, you cannot wear shoes, and so my shoes were outside. I wanted to put on my shoes and get out of there, but they circled around me and started shouting at me. It was a rainy day, and I put my raincoat in my arms and walked backwards toward where my shoes were. Those people were saying, "Why are you going? Where are you going? Wait, we are going to kill you." From their voices, I could tell that they were afraid. God put fear in their hearts, and they were not able to do any harm to me.

When I came to the bus stop, the people from my church were waiting for me. I realized that I forgot my Bible in the mosque. I said, "Wait a minute, I'm going to get my Bible."

They said, "No way, you're not going back there. We can buy many Bibles for you, don't go back. Those people are going to kill you."

One of our church members worked at a post office near the mosque, and the next day, the Muslim priest brought my Bible to the post office. My name was printed on the cover, and he asked my church member, "Do you know this person?"

He recognized my name and replied, "Oh, this is my pastor."

The Muslim priest said, "Your pastor? My people were going to kill him last night, but we were not able to do any harm to him, because the power of God was very strong on your pastor. I believe that your pastor is a man of God. Please tell your pastor that we will not harm him anymore, and your pastor doesn't have to be afraid of us."

The same day, one of our church members was working at the airport as a contractor fixing the runway. Two of the other workers were saying, "You know, yesterday, that Christian pastor came to our mosque, and we were going to kill him, but somehow God let this man go, and we were not able to do anything."

While they were talking, the contractor came to them and said, "What are you talking about?" They told him about the Christian man who visited their mosque, and he said, "That's my pastor." He was one of the church members who had been with me in the mosque that day. So those people got scared, because he had hired them to work for him.

From these two instances, we came to know that these Muslim people really wanted to kill us, but God did not allow them to kill us, because God always protects his people.

ELDER OF THE CHURCH DELIVERED FROM SMOKING AND DRINKING

I went to one village. In that village, there was a very well-known elder of the church who owned a lot of land and had a lot of friends. They used to come to his house, and they would all sit around and smoke and drink. He had a ten-year supply of tobacco and a drum full of liquor.

I was sitting in the bus going to that village, and all of the people on the bus were Hindus. I was the only Christian. They were all smoking, and I was feeling uncomfortable, because the bus was filled with smoke. I couldn't tell everyone to stop smoking, but there was a "no smoking" sign on the bus. So I pulled the chain to stop the bus.

The ticket collector came and said, "Why did you stop the bus?"

I said, "What does the sign say? No smoking. Everybody's smoking here. Tell them to stop smoking. Otherwise, tell them to go out to smoke, and then come in."

I was well-dressed, and he thought I might be some kind of supervisor. So he stopped the bus and told everyone to go outside and smoke.

One passenger asked me, "Where are you going?"

I told him the name of the village and the person with whom I would be staying.

He said, "Those people all smoke and drink, especially the house where you will be staying. What are you going to do?"

I said, "I have a message from the Lord. I believe that person will hear the message from God, and he will be transformed."

That night, I told that church elder what had happened. I said, "I told those people you will not be smoking or drinking anymore, and your life will be changed."

He said, "I have been smoking since I was eight years old, and I do not harm anyone. Even though I smoke and drink, I'm a good person. I'm also the elder of the church. Many pastors came to my house but never told me about not smoking. I treat them like kings and give them some money, and they go. They never tell me that smoking is bad."

I told him, "God called me to preach the word of God. I did not come to your house to collect money or have good food. I will tell you what the Bible says."

I gave him a couple of Bible scriptures while I was conducting the evening service in his house: 1 Corinthians 3:16-17 and 1 Corinthians 6:19-20.

After the service, he said to me, "I never heard anyone preaching on these scriptures in my church."

I said, "Your pastors might be smoking, and so they will skip these scriptures and will not preach this word. The word of God says you are the temple of the living God, and if anyone destroys the temple of the living God, God will destroy him. Jesus Christ purchased us by His own blood, and we are not our own. We should glorify God with our body, soul, and spirit, which belong to God."

He was very impressed, and he said, "I'm convinced that this is not good for me. I want to please God, but it is so difficult for me to give up this bad habit. If you could pray to God to take the smoking taste out of my mouth, I will never smoke."

I prayed for him and said, "There is nothing impossible with God."

He did not smoke that night, and early in the morning, he said to his servant, who came to bring him a smoking pipe, "Take that filthy smell out of here."

God set him free from his smoking and drinking habits. As I

promised to those people who were smoking in the bus, God did what I said. I thank God, and all the glory goes to God.

PREACHING IN THE HINDU TEMPLE

One day I was going to visit the church elder who gave up smoking and drinking. This time, instead of taking a bus, I took a train. After getting out of the train, I had to walk another five miles to get to the village. It was a hot, sunny day, and while I was walking, another man followed me and said to me, "You seem very religious. Are you a prophet?"

I said to him, "I am a servant of Jesus Christ, and He has called me to preach the gospel and heal the sick. I pray for people, and God is doing signs, wonders, and miracles."

He said, "Could you please come and pray for my village?"

I said, "Where is your village?"

He showed me that his village was on the way.

I said, "I cannot come now at noontime. I will come this evening."

When I went to see the church elder, I told him about what had happened on the way. The church elder's family told me, "That village is very dangerous. You cannot go there. Many British and American pastors tried to go there, and the villagers stoned them and kicked them out of their village. The men carry knives and swords with them everywhere."

I said to them, "I promised that man that I would go, and I have to keep my word. I am not afraid of dying. My life is in God's hands."

At about 7:30 in the evening, one of the church elder's sons gave me a ride in his tractor, took me to the border of the village, and left. Now I didn't know what to do, because I didn't know the name or address of the man who invited me. When I was entering the village, I saw a Hindu temple, and so I went to the temple priests.

"One of your villagers invited me to come and preach the gospel," I said. "Can we advertise in this village and tell everyone to come to the temple?"

The priests said, "Okay, we can do that." They sent some young people into the streets, banging on plates and telling people to come to the temple. In the meantime, I asked the priests if some people could play music while I was singing. They invited some musicians, and I sang some Christian songs in the Gujarati language. The temple was on higher ground, at least four feet higher than the surrounding area, and almost the whole village was standing in front of the temple.

I stopped singing and started preaching. I gave my brief testimony and told everyone what God was doing in my life. I told them that Jesus came and gave His life to save mankind, so that whoever believes in Him will have eternal life. As I was standing there and preaching, there were so many Hindu idols behind me. I pointed to those idols and said, "Look at these idols. They have mouths, feet, and hands, but they don't talk, walk or do anything. However, Jesus Christ is alive, and I am His servant. I am going to pray for you, and God is going to heal you and do miracles among you."

I preached for two to three hours, and it was getting late. I gave an invitation to the people to come forward so that I could pray for them. Many people gave many prayer requests, and God touched them and healed them.

At the same time, however, I heard some whispering. Since I knew the language, I understood what the people were saying. I asked them, "Are you trying to kill me?"

Some of them loudly responded, "Yes, we are going to kill you!"

I said, "I did not do any harm to you. I just prayed for you in the name of Jesus, and many of you are already blessed. If you kill me, tomorrow the police will come and arrest many of you, because I told the other village that I was coming here. If I don't come back, they will call the police, and the name of your village will be spoiled. If you want to keep your village's name, you can do something."

Some of the good people in the village, who had been blessed, said, "What should we do?"

I said, "Take me back to where I came from, because it is very dark, and I don't know the way to go back."

Somehow, those people agreed to take me back. There were almost twelve young men who took torches in their hands. Those were handmade torches, which were poles eight to ten feet tall, with the ends tightly wrapped in cloth, dipped in cooking oil, and lit on fire. They took a bucket of oil with them, in case the torches went out. By faith, I walked with them, praying in my heart that these people should not do any harm to me.

The Christians in the other village were waiting for me. When they saw the torches, they thought that maybe I had been killed, and these villagers were bringing my body. When I came closer, however, I shouted, "Praise the Lord! Hallelujah!"

The people who brought me said, "Can we go back now?"

I said, "You can go back. I'm so grateful that you brought me here safely."

This was really God's grace. Many people wanted to go to that village and could not preach the gospel there, but God gave me grace. I give glory and honor to God. As Paul said in Romans 1:16, "I am not ashamed of the gospel of Jesus Christ."

SNAKE BITE

It was a summer day, and it was very hot inside the house. I decided to sleep outside on the open porch. In the middle of the night, a cobra bit me on my leg. I was sound asleep, but when I felt some pain, I grabbed the heavy snake with one hand and threw it. It made a loud sound when it fell to the ground. Thank God that snake went away and did not come back to bite me again. I went inside, turned on the light, and saw what kind of wound it was. There were three holes in my leg, two on the top and one on the bottom.

There was a laundromat on the same plot of land, and the owner was pressing his clothes. I showed him the wound, and he said, "That is a snake bite." He didn't want to say so at first, because he was a Hindu, and he worshipped snakes. "There are so many snakes on my plot," he said. "I will arrange to have you taken to the hospital."

I said, "Please don't do that. I'm not going to the hospital. I believe God will heal me. If my time has come, no doctor can save my life."

Then he said, "Please do not sleep until 4:00, at least. If you sleep, you will die. Keep yourself awake."

I went inside, put some coconut oil on a cotton ball, placed it on the wound, and placed a bandage over it. It was 1:00, and I started praying. I was planning to pray until 4:00. However, I fell asleep and dreamed that I was seeing a clock on the wall that said 4:00, even though I didn't actually have a clock. That was my normal prayer time, and so I woke up and heard the laundromat owner's baby crying.

I had asked the laundromat owner earlier if I could pray for the baby. She was six months old and had a high fever. They had gone to the hospital and gotten medicine, but the baby was crying continuously.

The laundromat owner said to me, "You cannot pray for my child, because you have a snake bite." Hindu people believed that the snake was their god, and so they thought that their god might be punishing me. So the laundromat owner didn't want me to pray for the child.

When I woke up at 4:00, I went to the laundromat owner and said to him, "Your baby has been crying the whole night. Can I pray for her now?"

He was surprised to see me and said, "Are you still alive?"

I said, "By the grace of God, I am still alive, and, if you give me permission, I would like to pray for your baby."

This time, he was very happy and said, "Please come and pray for my baby."

I went to his house, laid hands on the baby and prayed in the name of Jesus. The baby stopped crying, and she was immediately healed. I give glory and honor to God.

The next morning, I took my bicycle and traveled twenty-two miles, preaching the gospel. When I returned, I removed the bandage and saw that I was completely healed, without medicine. Our God is a miracle-working God.

MY FIRST CAR FOR THE LORD'S WORK

I only had a bicycle for transportation, and I would travel sometimes between twenty and fifty miles. One day I went 120 miles. Can you imagine my body breaking while I was going here and there? I wanted to get a driver's license. I asked everyone if there was a driving school in the district. I was told that I would have to travel 120 miles to a different district in order to find a driving school. It would have been very expensive to travel such a long distance and stay in a hotel for a few weeks. So I prayed, "Lord, please open a driving school close to my church." I believed that God would hear my prayer.

One day, I took my bicycle and went for evangelistic work, passing out tracts and telling people about Jesus. I saw a jeep coming toward me with a driving school sign on the side. I stopped the jeep and asked the driver where the driving school was. He asked me if I was interested in learning to drive, and I said yes. We put my bicycle in his jeep, and he drove me to the driving school.

While he was driving, I noticed that he was from out of state. I started talking to him in his language, and he was very happy that someone knew his language.

"I'm going to introduce you to my boss as my friend," he said.

"That would be great," I said.

The driving school used to charge 250 rupees for a deposit and maybe twenty-five rupees per lesson. However, when he introduced me to his boss, I wasn't charged for a deposit, and I was only charged five rupees per lesson.

"When did you start the driving school?" I asked.

"Last week," they replied.

The driving school was within walking distance, and I was so thankful to God that He had heard my prayer immediately. By the grace of God, after four lessons, I was able to get my driver's license. Now I started praying that God would give me a car.

I was doing mission work three hundred miles away from my church. Someone invited me to his third floor apartment. People came to know that I was there, and they started coming for healing. When people got healed, this man was very surprised and happy.

"You are doing a great job," he said. "You need a car. I am a car dealer, and I'll show you a car. If you like it, you can have it." From his porch, he showed me a car that was parked on the street. It was a newly painted, beautiful, blue Studebaker Champion. Just looking at it, I liked it.

I said, "That looks beautiful."

The man said, "How much do you think it's worth?"

I thought, "Maybe fifteen thousand?"

He said, "You like it?"

I said, "I have to take a test drive, to make sure whether I like it."

We took a test drive, and I liked the car very much.

He said, "You want to buy this car?"

I said, "Sir, I have only twenty-five hundred in the bank that I'm saving for a motorcycle."

He said, "If you give me that money, I will give you this car."

I gave him the money from the bank. Since my church was

three hundred miles away, I said, "It's too far away to go, and I have no experience driving on highways."

He arranged for a driver, and he parked the car in front of my church. God did a miracle, and that's the way I got my first car.

five

✿

MIRACLES IN MY LIFE

When Jesus sent His disciples in Matthew 10:8, He said, "Heal the sick, cleanse the lepers, raise the dead, cast out devils: freely ye have received, freely give." Many people today, when they do the Lord's work, they charge you something. They tell you, "If you want to receive a blessing, give some money." Jesus said, "Freely ye have received, freely give." I never charged anyone for their healings yet, and I don't think I'm going to charge anyone for the rest of my life. Even though we had conventions and rented large town halls, we said, "Admission is free, and no collection will be taken in the services." That's the way I started my ministry.

No man can heal anyone without Christ. Jesus has called us to do His work. Jesus said in John 14:12, "He that believeth on Me, the works that I do shall he do also; and greater works than these shall he do; because I go unto My Father." Jesus did so many miracles. He turned water into wine. He healed the lame and the blind, and he cleansed lepers. He calmed the storms and walked on water. He fed more than five thousand people with five loaves and two fish. He raised the dead, even though Lazarus was dead and buried for four days. There are many miracles recorded in the Bible, yet some people say today, "Now, no more miracles can happen because Jesus is gone." As I mentioned above, Jesus said in John 14:12, "He that believeth on Me, the works that I do shall he do also; and greater works than these shall he do; because I go unto My Father."

People believe that we cannot do greater things than Jesus, but Jesus Christ was not lying. We see that Jesus Christ only worked in Israel, but today we have jet planes. We can go anywhere and preach the gospel. We have radio, television, satellite, and the internet. We have all kinds of facilities that Jesus didn't have, and so we are preaching the gospel in a greater way than Jesus did in those days.

Now, let's talk about miracles. Peter's shadow healed the sick. Paul's handkerchief was given to sick people, and they were healed. The church was established when Jesus sent the Holy Spirit on the Day of Pentecost, and Paul said that he was preparing the church for the return of Christ. These are works that Jesus didn't do, but He allowed us to do them. These are the greater works.

Jesus said in Revelation 1:18, "I am He that liveth, and was dead; and behold, I am alive forevermore." Jesus is alive, and we read in Hebrews 13:8, "Jesus Christ is the same yesterday, and today, and forever." That means Jesus Christ is an unchangeable God. He is alive today, and He is doing miracles in my life and the lives of many servants of God. If you believe Jesus Christ as your Lord and Savior, you will be saved and healed, and you will be doing miracles like Jesus did. The word of God says that we are the body of Christ. If we are the body of Christ, then we are His hands, His feet, and His mouth. We are the ones now here in this world to do miracles and healings and bring the message of salvation to the world.

David says in Psalm 40:5, "Many, O Lord my God, are thy wonderful works which thou hast done, and thy thoughts which are to us-ward: they cannot be reckoned up in order unto thee: if I would declare and speak of them, they are more than can be numbered." I feel the same way. If I start telling you all the miracles God did in my life, they will be many, but I'm going to tell you a few small and great miracles God did for me.

FINANCIAL NEEDS MET

One day, I went for shopping to buy some cooking oil. In those days, you would bring your own bottle or container to buy oil. I had a small bottle, maybe eight to ten ounces, and I told the man to fill it. He filled the bottle and told me the amount, but when I checked in my pocket, I had one penny less than I needed to pay for it.

I said, "Could you remove one penny's worth of oil?"

The seller told me, "I cannot do that. You can give me a penny next time you come for shopping."

I just turned around, and there was a penny on the floor. So I said, "Here is a penny," and gave him a penny. I thank God that I didn't have to owe anyone, not even a penny.

One day, I was praying for ten dollars. There was a knock at the door in the evening, and the person at the door said, "You gave me ten dollars a long time ago, and I was always thinking to give you these ten dollars." God is so faithful. He will give you exactly what your need is.

I had an invitation to go to one convention. I thought I had enough money, and I went to the railway station to buy a ticket. However, the ticket master told me that I didn't have enough money. He insulted me and told me to leave.

When I got home, I started praying. I said, "Lord, if it's not your will that I should go, then I don't have to go." I started unpacking my bag, but I felt in my spirit that God wanted me to go to the convention.

I went back to the railway station, sat on a bench, and prayed. Some of my church members came to know that I was going, and they went there to meet me. They started shaking my hand

and giving me cash for my journey. By the grace of God, I now had three to four times more than the ticket master was asking. I even had money for a return ticket. I gave the money to one of the church members and asked him to purchase a ticket for me. I didn't want to face that ticket master again. I thank God that He supplied my need in due time.

One day, I had been preaching the gospel in one town and wanted to leave, but I had only one dime remaining in my pocket. No one had taken an offering for me, and I did not tell anyone that I needed money. I went to the railway station and opened my bag, and there was an envelope inside filled with money. I thanked God, purchased my ticket, and went on my journey.

One time I was praying for twenty thousand dollars, and someone gave me a check for twenty thousand dollars. From a penny to thousands of dollars, there is nothing impossible with God. Philippians 4:19 says, "But my God shall supply all your need according to his riches in glory by Christ Jesus."

LOST AND FOUND

One lady called me from New York. She said, "Someone told me that God listens to your prayers. So I have a prayer request. I have very bad diabetes. I'm taking all of the medicines and everything, but it is not going away."

I said, "I'm going to pray. If you believe, God is going to heal you." I gave her some Bible scriptures to encourage her faith, and I prayed that God would take away her diabetes and heal her completely. After prayer, I told her to say, "I receive my healing by faith," and she believed it. I told her, "Now you are healed by faith. Go for a check-up, and they will not find any diabetes in your blood."

She called me later and said, "I went for a check-up, and there is no trace of diabetes in my blood. I am cured."

I said, "Thank God. God heard our prayer. You are healed. Now go and tell someone what Jesus Christ has done for you."

Then she said, "I have one more prayer request. My son disappeared in New York City for twenty-five years. I tried everything but could not find him. Since you prayed for me and my faith is increased, I believe that if you pray that my son should come home, he will come home. I was going to do a pretend funeral for him."

I said, "Hebrews 4:13 says there is nothing hidden in God's eyes; everything is open and naked to his eyes. That means He knows where your son is. I'm going to pray, and if your son is alive, he will come home."

I prayed, "Lord, if her son is alive, let him come home."

Later on, the lady called me again and said, "Pastor Peter, guess what?"

I said, "Your son came home?"

She said, "How did you know?"

I said, "Didn't we pray that your son should come home?"

She said, "We are having a party. My son is home."

I said, "Tell him that we prayed for him, and God brought him home."

I told this story to my congregation in the Sunday service, and one grandmother said to me, "Pastor Peter, I have a prayer request. My son died, and his wife took my grandchildren and went away. I don't know where she is and where my grandchildren are. Almost ten years have passed, and I would not even recognize my grandchildren. Please pray that God will allow me to see my grandchildren someday."

I gave her the same Bible scripture, Hebrews 4:13, and I prayed with her that God would bring her grandchildren and that she would be able to see them.

After the service, she was standing at the bus stop when a boy and girl, ages fourteen and twelve, came up to her and said, "Grandma, grandma," but she did not recognize them. Those children started saying their father's name, their mother's name, and even their grandmother's name. They gave their names, and then she recognized them. The following Sunday, she brought those children to the Sunday service and testified that God heard our prayer.

There was another mother listening to her testimony. She said, "I heard the testimony about the lady from New York, and now I heard this testimony. Could you please pray for me? My daughter disappeared many years ago. I don't know where she is."

I gave her the same scripture, Hebrews 4:13, and I said, "If God did it for these two families, He can do it for you also." I prayed with her that her daughter would come and see her.

She went home after the service, and she called me. She said, "Someone called me from New York and said that she saw my daughter. She did not give me any more information, and she hung up the phone. So now I am more confused."

I said, "Mother, you didn't know if your daughter was dead or alive. Now you heard that she is alive. Just thank God. There is nothing impossible with God. You will see your daughter pretty soon." I prayed with her again that her daughter should come and see her.

Pretty soon, her daughter came to see her, and I thank God that He heard my prayer.

CHILDREN ARE A GIFT FROM GOD

There are so many people today who cannot have children. Let me give you a few examples of how God enabled some women to have children when it was said to be impossible.

In India, if you cannot have children, people look down on you, and ladies become so depressed if they cannot have children. One Christian lady introduced me to a Hindu lady who was married for many years without any children. The Hindu lady said to me, "Could you please pray for me, so that I will have a child? If I have a child, I will give the child a Christian name, and I will tell everyone that Jesus gave this child to me." I prayed for her in the name of Jesus, and the following year she gave birth to a son.

I prayed for a Christian nurse who was hemorrhaging, and God healed her. She said to me, "Since you prayed for me and God healed me, I believe that if you pray for my sister, she will have children. She is married to a medical doctor, and since twelve years, they have been trying to have children with no success."

"There is nothing impossible with God," I said. "I will pray for her, and she will have children."

She was two to three thousand miles away from us. I told the nurse, "Tell your sister to stay in her room and pray. You stay in your room and pray, and I'll stay in the church and pray." Matthew 18:19-20 says that if two people agree on earth and pray, God will hear their prayer, and if three people are united, God's presence will be there. According to these words, I said, "God will hear our prayer." We prayed together, and pretty soon, the lady got her first son. All the glory goes to God.

We were having weekly prayer meetings in the home of one Christian family. The lady of the house, who was almost forty years old, told me that, every time she became pregnant, she would have a miscarriage. I told her that I would pray to God that He would give her a child, and that she would not have a miscarriage this time. Pretty soon, she was pregnant, and she was very excited. I asked her to tell me her due date, so that I could keep praying for her safe delivery. It so happened that, on that date, I was on a mission trip. In the middle of the night, I remembered her, and I knelt and prayed for her safe delivery. Thank God, she delivered a baby girl, without any complications. When I returned from my trip, everyone was happy that God heard our prayer.

We continued to have weekly prayer meetings in their house, and after four years, she had not given birth to any more children.

Although they never asked me to pray for another child, I asked God to give them a son. A year later, she delivered a baby boy.

"What should we name this son?" they asked me.

"You didn't ask me to name the first child," I said. "You can name him whatever you want."

However, they insisted, "Please give us a name."

"I have a name in my heart," I said, "but you tell me whatever name you have in mind."

"We were thinking of Samuel," they said.

I was thinking of the same name, and so they were very happy. Both children were healthy, without any deformity. The glory goes to God.

There was a born again Christian lady who used to live across from our church. She came to our church and said, "I have an eleven-year-old daughter. She wants a brother or sister. I believe that, if you pray for me, God will give me children."

I prayed for her in the name of Jesus and said to her, "Get ready. God is going to give you children." She believed what I said and started preparing a crib. Pretty soon, she became pregnant, and she moved to Texas, where she worked as a registered nurse.

Years passed, and one of her friends visited our church. I asked her, "Your friend went to Texas. Do you have any news from her? How many children does she have?"

She said, "To tell you the truth, I lost count."

Thank God, our God is a prayer-answering God.

One day, a mother and daughter visited our church. The daughter said to me, "I am always having miscarriages. I heard that you prayed for one sister who was pregnant and had a tumor, and God healed her and gave her a healthy baby. So I believe that if you pray for me, God will give me children."

To increase her faith, I told her a couple of stories about how God did miracles, and I prayed for her.

She called me one day and said, "I am six months pregnant

now, but I started bleeding. This is what happens each time I get pregnant."

I said, "Remember I prayed that this time you will not get a miscarriage."

By the grace of God, she had a full pregnancy and, without any complications, she delivered her first child. Later, she had another child, without any complications. Our God is a prayer-answering God.

One young couple in our church was married for seven years, but they never told me that they wanted children. They were a very healthy and joyful couple. They both loved the Lord. One day, her mother invited me to their house. When I went there, she started explaining to me, "My daughter has been married for seven years, and she doesn't have any children. Both of them went to the doctor, but the doctor said that both of them could not have children. But if you pray, God will hear your prayer, and they will have children."

I laid hands on her daughter's stomach and I prayed that they would have children. I said, "If God gives you a son, dedicate him for the Lord's work," and she agreed. By the grace of God, she had a son, without any complications. They continued coming to our church.

Later on they decided to leave our church and go to a bigger church so that their child would have more facility to play around. So I said, "It's up to you," and they went to a bigger church. I did not recommend them. They went on their own. I don't know the pastor's name. I don't know the church name.

A couple of years later, the lady called me. She was so depressed and upset. She started telling me that she went to her pastor and asked him to pray for another child. The pastor said, "I don't have faith like Pastor Peter." (From that, I understood that pastor didn't believe in miracles.) He told them to go to the doctor. The husband and wife went to the doctor and took the doctor's advice, and afterward she was bleeding and hurting.

She said, "Pastor Peter, I made a mistake going to the doctor."

I said, "You know, in the beginning you went to the doctor, and the doctor said you could not have children. God did a miracle and gave you a son. Why didn't you ask God to give you another child?"

She said, "Could you please pray for me?"

I prayed for her, and God gave her a daughter. The glory goes to Jesus Christ.

There was a Christian lady who was nine months pregnant, and she went to the hospital for a check-up. The doctor told her that her baby was dead. She told him to remove the dead baby, but he said, "Go home, and I'll call you. Other ladies are waiting for delivery." Twenty-four hours passed, but the doctor never called her. She was concerned that the poison from the dead baby's body would go to her heart and she would die also. She was afraid and crying when I met her. I asked her why she was crying, and she told me what had happened.

"Do you know the story of Lazarus?" I asked her. "Lazarus was dead for four days, and Jesus raised him. The same Jesus can raise your baby from the dead. There is nothing impossible with God. I'm going to pray for you, and your baby will be alive."

I laid my hand on her stomach and prayed that God would raise that child from the dead. After prayer, I told her, "Please go to another hospital and another doctor. Don't go to the same place. Your baby is alive, and you will have a safe delivery."

She believed what I said and went for her delivery. She delivered a healthy baby girl. All the glory goes to God. Jesus Christ says, "I am the resurrection and the life."

God did a miracle, but you have to believe and receive things by faith. Even if somebody tells you something is impossible, you have to believe there is nothing impossible with God.

GOD'S DIVINE PROTECTION

The word of God says in John 10:10, "The thief cometh not, but for to steal, and to kill, and to destroy: I am come that they might have life, and that they might have it more abundantly." I have experienced this in my life. I believe that the devil is there to destroy, but that Jesus is here to give life and more abundant life. I'm going to tell you how God protected me from the enemy's hand.

One day, I was preaching the gospel of Jesus Christ on the beach in Bombay City, and many people were quietly listening, except for one husky man who showed his fist and came running toward me. I was not afraid, however; I just stood there and kept on preaching. The man was about five feet in front of me when his feet became entangled in the sand. He fell down and was not able to get up. I asked the people around him to help him up. He was ashamed and quietly walked away. If this man would have punched me, I would not have had the strength to defend myself. I was the lone Christian there, with no one else to help me, but God protected me.

One family invited me to preach in their village. As I was going, some of the Christian brothers and sisters said, "We'll come with you." So we went there, and I started preaching in the evening. It was an outdoor meeting, and there was a line of haystacks ten feet high. I thought this would be a good backdrop, as it would provide some protection as I was preaching. However, some bad person, with a knife in his hand, climbed up a haystack, looking for an opportunity to jump on me, but no one noticed him, as they were paying attention to my preaching. Since there was no podium, I was walking around on stage. Because I wasn't standing still, he had a hard time trying to jump on me. Instead, he fell down in front of me and ran away in the dark, and no one was able to catch him.

We decided to close the service with prayer, and we left. It was nighttime, and we had no transportation to return home. If we walked home, surely those people would kill us on the way. We walked to the highway, where there were no buses traveling, only large trucks.

I said to the people, "If any truck comes, I'm going to stop the truck."

They said to me, "It's dangerous. No one will stop in this highway."

I said to them, "God will protect me and help us to get home."

I stood in front of an oncoming truck and waved my hands, and the truck stopped.

The truck driver said to me, "Why are you in the middle of the street? You would have been killed."

I said, "Sir, we have no transportation. Could you give us a ride?"

The truck driver agreed, and everyone got safely inside the truck. As we were getting inside, we saw a mob of people running toward us carrying sticks and knives, but as the truck drove away, they were not able to catch up to us. By the grace of God, the driver took us safely home.

You can see how God's hand is in our lives when we are preaching the gospel of Jesus Christ. The word of God says, "I will never leave you nor forsake you." 2 Timothy 1:7 says that God has not given us a spirit of fear, but He has given us power, love, and a sound mind. Deuteronomy 28:7 says that the enemy will come one way but will flee seven ways.

I was going on a mission trip, and it was an eight-hour journey. I was traveling by train, riding in a large compartment that seated about a hundred people. Early in the morning, four police officers and a sergeant entered with a man whose hands and feet were chained. The officers remained standing as the man was seated across from me. He sat quietly, looking depressed. The law was that prisoners were not allowed to speak, and the public was not allowed to speak to them. However, I knew that this would be my only chance to talk to this man before he was taken to prison, and God inspired me to talk to him.

"Where are these people taking you?" I asked.

"To the death penalty," he said.

"You might have done horrible things," I said.

"Yes," he said, "I did all kinds of things. Now they're taking me to jail, and I'm going to die there."

"Listen, I have a good story to tell you," I said. "Jesus Christ came from heaven and died on the cross of Calvary for you and your sins. If you confess your sins to Jesus Christ and ask forgiveness, He will forgive all your sins. He will wash your sins away, and you will be clean inside. Jesus Christ will give you eternal life. Even if you ask the police or government to pardon you, in this situation, they are not going to forgive you. They are not going to release you. Jesus Christ said, 'Ye shall know the truth, and the truth shall set you free.'"

As I was preaching to this man, his face lit up. "I believe," he said. He wanted to believe and listen more.

I was about to lead him in a sinner's prayer for salvation, but the police officers stopped me. "Stop preaching to this man," they told me, "otherwise we will arrest you."

"What did I do?" I said. "I was just telling him about Jesus."

"We don't want to hear it," they said.

I was the only Christian in that whole compartment. Everyone else was Hindu, but no one opposed me, except for the police officers.

"See?" I said to the man. "I am not even a criminal, and these people want to harass me. It's no wonder that, with what you have done, they are not going to release you. If you give your heart to Jesus Christ, your sins will be forgiven, and you will be a free man inside. If you die, you will go to heaven."

That man was excited, but the police officers started harassing me. One of them said, "Our sergeant has the power to make you vomit blood and kill you, sitting on that seat now. You won't be able to get up, and you will be vomiting blood."

"Sir," I said, "I serve Jesus, who is the living God. The Bible teaches me that God is love. God sent His Son to die on the cross of Calvary for the whole world. The word of God says in John 3:16, 'For God so loved the world, that He gave His only begotten Son, that whosoever believeth in Him should not perish but have everlasting life.' What kind of god are you serving that wants to kill people and make them vomit blood?"

I was standing up by now. "Listen," I said to the people, "now these are two powers. My God is love, and their god is a destroyer. Which one do you want?"

The police officers became much more angry at me, but God gave me holy boldness to talk to the sergeant.

"Can you make me vomit blood right now in front of these people?" I asked him.

"I can't do anything right now," he said. "I'm on duty."

I said, "Sir, I know the Bible says the greater One is within me than what is in the world. My God is greater than any gods or any devil. You can set a time and place, I'll announce it on radio and in the newspapers, and everyone can come and see you make me vomit blood."

The police officers became so embarrassed that they left my compartment.

I am not afraid of anyone or anything, because Jesus Christ lives in me. I am not here to hurt somebody. I am here to help somebody, to bring people to the saving knowledge of Jesus Christ. I am doing the Lord's work, not by might, not by power, but by the spirit of the Lord. I know for sure He has called me with a definite high calling.

I was driving at night, and I had a passenger with me. I was talking to him about Jesus. "Any accident can happen on the highway," I said to him. "I'm ready to go to heaven. How about you?"

"Oh, I'm not ready," he said.

"If you believe Jesus Christ, you will be saved, and God will protect you," I said, but he did not want to hear anything.

As I was driving, another car was approaching, and my headlights were really bright. I didn't want to blind the other driver, and so I tried to dim the headlights. However, I accidentally turned the headlights off, and so I could not see where I was going.

The light switch was closer to the passenger side, and so I asked my passenger to turn the headlights back on.

"I don't know anything about cars," he said. "Do it yourself."

When I leaned over to turn the light switch, the car tilted, and we started going down a hill. We finally stopped when the car hit a tree; otherwise, we would have gone all the way down the hill and into the river below. My passenger started crying for help, but there was no one to help us in the middle of the night.

"Nothing is going to happen to us," I said, "because God is with us."

We did not know where we were, because it was pitch dark, and the car door on my side was blocked by bushes, so that I was not able to open it. I asked my passenger to open his door, but he did not want to get out of the car. So I opened the window and climbed out. I was scratched by a thorn bush on the way out, but neither of us were seriously hurt. The next morning, I could see from the highway that my car was off the side of the road, about twenty-five feet down, closer to the river. If we had gone a little bit further, we might have completely drowned, but God protected us.

I would advise you that, before you start your car, you should pray and ask for God's protection. God will protect you, if you are a born-again child of God. Lay your hand on your car before you get into it, and say, "Lord, be my driver, and I just want You to take control of my car." If you drive that way, God will protect you. Hebrews 1:14 says that, when you are a born-again child of God, God sends His angels to protect you. That's the way God protected me.

God knows how to protect His people from all the dangers and harms. I'm telling you as a living witness. I believe that God has a timing for us. When our time has come, we will be gone, but as long as God keeps you in this world, keep on doing God's work.

CASTING OUT DEMONS

In the name of Jesus, people can be healed, delivered and set free. Not only that, Jesus Christ said in Mark 16:17, "And these signs shall follow them that believe; in my name shall they cast out devils." There are so many people who don't even believe in demons. But I tell you, there are real demons in this world, and the devil is real. God gave me grace to pray for demon-possessed people. I'll give a couple of examples of what God did through this ministry in my life.

There was a Hindu lady who was brought to my church for prayer. She was sitting in the church and harassing other people. I told her to stop, and I said, "After the service, I will pray for you." I did not know what was wrong with her, but I prayed for her in the name of Jesus. The lady went home and cooked dinner at her house for the first time in a long while. That evening, someone told me that this lady had a demon, and her family used to chain her because she was bothering other people. This was a great miracle for the family, and that's why someone came and testified about what God had done. Even though I didn't know that lady was demon-possessed, God knew, and He gave me grace to cast that demon out. I give glory to Jesus Christ.

One day, my father arranged a special healing service. While we were praising God, one lady stood there, uncovered her hair, and started acting unmannerly. I knew in my spirit that she might be demon-possessed. I laid my hand on her head and rebuked the evil spirit. She fell on her face and, a few minutes later, stood up and testified that she had seven demons but was now completely free. After the service, many people were saved. I baptized many people, and she was one of them.

On a Monday morning, two men came to my church with their friend. He was an educated Hindu Brahman who worked as a treasurer for a large company. They told me, "This man is demon-possessed. Sometimes, an attack comes to him, and he acts all weird."

I said to him, "Listen, you need freedom? Jesus Christ is going to set you free. There is power in the blood of Jesus Christ. Can you say, 'the blood of Jesus Christ'?"

He said, "I cannot say that word."

I said, "Look at me then."

He was looking down and said, "I cannot look at your face."

From all of this, I understood that he was really demon-possessed. I said to his friends, "I am going to cast the demon out in the name of Jesus. Keep the door open and let the demon go, or else he will jump on you."

I laid my hand on that man's head, and I rebuked the demon and told him to get out of that man. The man fell on his face, and a white foam came out of his mouth. Then he got up and started testifying. He said, "There was someone inside me, twisting me. As soon as you prayed, he came out, and I saw him going out the door."

That man was a completely different person now. He talked very nicely with me. I asked him, "Can you say 'blood of Jesus' now?" and he repeated it after me. I told him to say there is power in the blood of Jesus, and I told him to invite Jesus into his heart and ask forgiveness for his sins. He gladly did, and he invited me to his office, where he would tell others about what Jesus did for him.

One day, a Christian lady who went to our church said to me, "In my house, there is a man and his son. He is a married man, about twenty-five years old, but all of a sudden something happened to him. He doesn't talk. He doesn't communicate with anyone, and he is not deaf and dumb." This family lived miles away, but she asked them to stay at her house while she invited me to come and pray for him.

I went with her to pray for him. I put my hand on his head and rebuked that dumb spirit. As soon as I prayed for him, he was delivered from that demonic spirit, and he became completely normal. I talked with him, and we had a good conversation. He and his father went home rejoicing. Our God is a miracle-working God.

There was a church that sent missionaries to Africa, but somehow one lady who went with the missionaries became demon-possessed. When they came back, their ministers prayed to cast the demon out of her but had no success. This lady was not talking, praying, reading the Bible, or even smiling. One of the pastors invited me to the church to pray for her, because they knew that, in my ministry, many people were being healed, delivered, and set free. Even though that church was one of the largest churches in the city, and they had several pastors, they were not able to cast that demon out.

"Christian people cannot be demon-possessed. Maybe that lady went for a mission trip, and she was not even born again," I said. "I'll come and pray for that lady."

When I went there, I told these pastors to stand in a circle surrounding that lady. I stepped inside the circle of pastors, laid my hand on the lady's head, and commanded that demon to go out of her in Jesus' name. After prayer, I said to the lady, "Just praise God." She lifted both her hands and started praising God. I told her to re-dedicate her life to God, and she did. She started singing and reading the Bible. She became like a new person. After that, many people started coming from that church to our healing services.

Our God is a miracle-working God, and He has given us the same power. Jesus said in John 14:12, "He that believeth on me, the works that I do shall he do also; and greater works than these shall he do, because I go unto my Father." Many people do not believe this scripture, but what Jesus said is true. If you believe what Jesus said, you will be doing the same things that Jesus did. I just want to encourage you not to be afraid of any devil, because "greater is he that is in you, than he that is in the world" (1 John 4:4).

six

⚜

MIRACULOUS HEALINGS

Miracles are happening all the time. Sometimes people write to us in various parts of the world, and we are not able to go to their houses and talk to them or lay hands on them. However, the word of God says in Psalm107:20, "He sent His word, and healed them, and delivered them from their destructions." There is a power in the word of God. God is able to send His word and heal you.

SKIN DISEASES HEALED

We were holding a weekly cottage meeting in the home of a Christian family. The youngest daughter had a skin condition on her legs. After the meeting, she asked me to pray for her skin problem.

"Give me some oil," I said. "I will pray over the oil in Jesus' name. Apply the oil, and you will be healed."

The following week, she said to me, "I didn't get healed. Touch me and pray for me, and I will be healed."

She was almost fifteen or sixteen years old, and I did not

want to touch her. However, she insisted, and so I told her family, "Please keep your eyes open while I pray."

I prayed for her, and the following week she testified that she was healed overnight. By the grace of God, she and most of her sisters were saved and baptized, and the glory goes to God.

We had a healing service in one town. Many people were being healed. One person came wearing a bedsheet. She asked me to pray for her skin problems. Her skin was completely red all over, and she could not wear any clothes. That's why she was wearing a bedsheet. There was not a single place on her skin that I could lay hands and pray. I laid my hands on the floor and asked her to step on my hands.

"You are a servant of God," she said. "I cannot step on your hands."

"Sister," I said, "only your feet have no redness. So I believe that if you step on my hands, the power of God will heal you."

She stood on my hands, and I prayed for her.

"Please come tomorrow," I told her.

The next day in the prayer line, she came with a beautiful, blue sari and matching blouse with golden embroidery. She had completely healthy skin. When her turn came, I asked her, "Sister, what can I do for you?"

"Yesterday, you prayed for me," she said, "and God completely healed me. Look at my skin."

I asked her, "Since how long were you having this skin problem?"

"Since forty years," she said.

I didn't want to embarrass her, but I said, "Can I ask how old you are now?"

"I am forty-five years old," she said, but she looked very young to me after she had been healed.

Can you imagine this sister's life? From the time that she was a five-year-old child, she had suffered for forty years, but all of this forty-year problem disappeared overnight. No doctor or medicine was able to heal her, but Jesus healed her instantly.

I was having healing crusades in many places. I was just walking in the main street, and one lady came shouting, "Preacher, preacher!"

I stopped and said, "What can I do for you?"

"I attended one of your healing services," she said. "Many people were getting healed, and so I stood in line for prayer. I had a skin disease, white and brown spots all over my body. After you prayed, overnight my skin completely changed. Now I have skin like baby's skin."

I reminded her, "I am not the healer. I prayed in the name of Jesus, and Jesus healed you. Thank you for testifying and telling me what God has done for you." I was so thankful to God for doing healings and miracles in our services. All glory goes to Jesus Christ.

One of my church members came to me and said, "I have a Hindu neighbor. He and his family have a very bad skin disease. They tried everything to treat their disease, and nothing is helping. I told him that you could come and pray for them, and all of them will be completely healed."

I went to their house and told them, "I am going to pray for you in the name of Jesus. If you agree and believe, you will be healed. Give me a little bottle of oil, and I will pray over it. Apply that oil to everyone, and you will be healed."

They said, "We have twenty to forty gallons of oil. Pray over this oil, and we are going to take a bath in this oil."

I told them that they didn't need this much oil, but they insisted. So I prayed over the oil, and I left. The whole family, the father, mother, and their several children, took a bath in that oil. Overnight, their skin became worse. My church member came to me and told me that his neighbor had complained that their condition had become worse after I prayed for them.

"Don't worry," I said. "That disease is coming out, and they will be completely healed. There won't be any skin problem. I believe that God heard my prayer."

Mark 11:24 says, "What things soever ye desire, when ye pray, believe that ye receive them, and ye shall have them." I had that kind of faith.

A couple of weeks later, I was standing on the local railway station platform, waiting for my train. A lady who was holding a child came up to me and said, "Do you recognize me? My whole family had skin disease, and we were suffering for a long time. You came to our house and prayed over our oil. Do you remember that?"

"I remember," I said. "Did you go to the hospital after we prayed?"

"No," she said, "we couldn't even leave the house, but after three days we were all healed. Look at my skin. Look at my child's skin. None of us have any scars. The whole family is completely healed."

"Thank you very much for testifying about what the Lord did for you," I said.

When my train came, I left and never saw her again, but I thank God for what He did for that family. Even though the enemy tried to scare that family, I didn't lose my faith.

One man came to me, standing far away from me. "I'm a leper!" he shouted. "Could you please pray for me?"

I was so scared of this disease when I was young. Some of you may not know about leprosy. There are two kinds of leprosy. One kind of leprosy causes white and brown spots all over the body. The other kind of leprosy causes people to lose their nose, ears, fingers, and toes, and the person becomes deformed. They also lose any sensation of pain. There was no cure at that time. This man had the second kind of leprosy.

"Come close," I said. "I'm going to lay hands and pray for you." I never prayed for a leper before, but I read in the word of God that Jesus touched lepers, cleansed them and healed them. I believed that if I did the same as Jesus did, the man would be healed. I had no doubt, and I prayed for him.

"God has already healed you," I told him. "Go in peace." The man walked away by faith, without asking questions, thankful that I had prayed for him.

However, the devil started putting doubt in my heart. My hands started tingling. I washed them with soap and water a couple of times, but the tingling would not go away. Then I knew that this was the devil's trick to discourage me from praying for people. The Bible says, "Resist the devil, and he will flee from you," and so I rebuked the devil, in the name of Jesus. Afterward, that tingling sensation, and that fear, went away.

Later on, I met that man again. This time, he did not have any deformity. "Can you recognize me?" he said. "I was the one having the disease of leprosy. Now look at my fingers. I make my own dough. I am completely healed. Could you please pray for me, so that I can get a job?" I was so thankful that God did a miracle for him, and that he testified about what God had done.

Our God is a miracle-working God. Leprosy is the worst kind of skin disease. If God can heal a leper, He can heal anyone. There is nothing impossible with God.

LEG PROBLEMS HEALED

I went for a cottage meeting, and there was one lady whose son had no bones in his legs. That lady was crying, telling me that her mother-in-law was harassing her because she gave birth to such a child. The boy was almost four years old. When I saw that child, I told the mother, "God is going to heal your child." I prayed over some oil and applied it to the boy. Nothing happened, but I told the mother to apply oil and pray over her boy every day in Jesus' name, and to believe that her son would walk someday. That lady believed and was encouraged. Later, someone told me that child was healed and running around, without any doctor's help.

I was having prayer meetings, and people would line up for healing. One night I dreamed that a little girl, maybe eight years old, was in the line for prayer, with her foot twisted upside down. In my dream, I prayed for that girl. The girl's leg turned around, and she was completely healed. After that, I started looking in the prayer lines to see if there was a girl like that coming for prayer. Here came that girl, with her mother and grandmother. I saw that her foot was twisted upside down. I remembered my dream, and I had faith that this girl would be healed right now. I told the mother and grandmother, "Jesus Christ is going to heal this girl right now, and you are going to see the miracle of God." I laid my hands on the girl's foot and prayed in the name of Jesus. I opened my eyes, because I wanted to see that miracle, and I saw with my own eyes that foot twisting and becoming right. I said to the mother and grandmother, "Look, look what God is doing for your daughter," and that child was completely healed.

I was having a healing service, and I was praying for people. One man came, walking bow-legged, and I prayed for him in the name of Jesus and told him, "You are going to walk straight." Months later, I was walking in the marketplace, and I saw this man coming straight toward me.

I recognized him, and I stopped him as he was walking. I began to walk bow-legged and asked him, "Did you walk like this before?"

"Yes," he said.

"What happened?" I asked him.

He said, "I went to a healing service, and one man prayed for me and told me that one day I would walk straight."

"I was that man, but you didn't recognize me," I said. "Do you know who healed you?"

He said, "I know Jesus healed me."

I was thanking God, because if this man wasn't the right

person, I could have gotten into trouble. Our God is a good God, and He answers prayer.

I was on a mission trip, and I went to one city. Near the railway station, there was a beautiful church. I thought in my heart, "It will be very good if I can rent this place for a healing service."

I went to the church and asked the pastor, "Can I use this place for a healing service?"

He said, "We are three different denominations using this building. I cannot say yes. I have to take permission from the other two pastors."

I asked all three pastors and, thank God, they gave me permission to conduct a healing service in that church, and they did not charge me anything. However, I could not do any advertisement because this was my first time in that city and I didn't know anyone there. So I decided to go into the neighborhood and tell people that there was a three-day meeting at this church.

I saw one house with a picture of Jesus on the front door, and so I thought that this was a Christian family. I knocked at the door, and a woman came to the door. I said, "Mother, we are going to have a healing service in your neighborhood. Please come, and if anyone is sick, please bring them also."

She said, "I'm a Catholic, and I don't go to any Protestant church." She was nasty, and I walked away.

On the first day of the service, God healed many people. It became nighttime, and I didn't know any hotel or other place to go in the city. However, after the service, one gentleman came and asked me, "Would you like to come to my house to stay?" He had a big bungalow with three or four servants. He gave me a room where I could stay, with food and everything.

I had three successful days of services in that church. I was going back to my headquarters the following morning, but while I was going, one man stood in front of me and said, "You have to come to my house."

I said, "Sir, if I come, I will miss my train, and if I miss my train, there won't be another train until the next day."

He said, "My house is not too far. Please come, and you will not miss the train."

I thought in my heart, "Jesus never turned anyone down. Why am I telling this person that I cannot come?" I felt guilty and asked the Lord for forgiveness in my heart, and I told the man that I would come to his house.

When I went to the man's house, I saw that his brother's leg was withered, and he was not able to bend it. I was in a hurry and said, "I'm going to pray for this brother. I'm going to miss my train."

His mother said, "Please wait. I'm going to bring my daughter. She works at the hospital. She has a stiff neck."

I was thinking, "If I wait for that lady to bring her daughter, my train will be gone." So I prayed in my heart, "Lord, please hold that train," and I waited.

When her daughter came, I prayed for her first. She was instantly healed, and she went back to work. Next, I was going to pray for the man with the withered leg. As I touched his leg, I could feel that there was a cigarette package in his pocket.

I said, "I am going to pray for you. God is going to heal you. You saw how God did a miracle for your sister. You have to give up this smoking habit. God will give you grace."

This man received Jesus Christ as his Lord and Savior, and he promised to give up cigarettes without any hesitation. I laid hands on his thigh and prayed in the name of Jesus. I told the man to sit seven times, and he said, "I cannot bend my leg, or it will break."

I said to him, "I already prayed. God already healed you."

He sat down seven times without any pain, and he was completely healed. His mother started crying.

I said, "Mother, why are you crying? Your daughter and your son got healed."

She said, "I feel sorry that you came to my house and invited me, and I rejected you. Could you forgive me?"

Then I remembered that this was the Catholic lady whom I had invited earlier. Her mouth was red with chewing tobacco and some green leaves which were addictive.

I told her, "I am going to pray for you, but you have to repent of your sins and give up this addictive stuff, and God will bless you." She willingly received Jesus Christ as her Lord and Savior. I believe there was joy in that house, and I left, praying that God would hold that train for me.

When I came to the train station, I learned that the train was delayed for two hours, and by the grace of God, I got that train. As I sat on the train, I thanked God for how he blessed me, supplied all my needs, and gave me victory in everything.

There was a young man admitted into the hospital. He was Hindu and became Christian. The doctor told him that he had bone cancer in his thigh and that his leg would have to be amputated. When his relatives heard this, they blamed him, saying that their god was cursing him because he had become a Christian.

I didn't know this man, but because someone told me about him, I went to visit him in the hospital. He tried to explain to me what happened to him. I said to him, "The Bible says in John 10:10 that the enemy comes to steal, kill, and destroy, but Jesus came to give us more abundant life. Jesus is going to touch and heal you, and all of your relatives will be surprised."

I laid hands on him and prayed for him in the name of Jesus. I asked him, "Do you have any pain right now?"

He said, "I don't have any pain at all."

I said, "That means Jesus Christ has already healed you. Call the doctor and tell him to do another X-ray, because this is your body. They cannot amputate your leg without your permission. They have to do another X-ray. I will come tomorrow and see you."

When I came the next day to see him, he was jumping for joy.

He said to me, "The doctor did the X-ray. I have no trace of cancer. I'm going home."

I said, "Our God is a miracle-working God. Go and tell everyone what Jesus Christ has done for you."

TUMORS DISAPPEARED

One lady came to our church. She had a tumor in the back of her head. I laid hands on her head, rebuked that tumor in the name of Jesus, and told her that her tumor was healed. God healed her, and she started coming regularly to church.

Five or six years later, she could not come to church because she was old and could not take the bus anymore. One day she called me and said, "Pastor Peter, I have some heaviness in the back of my head." She was thinking that maybe the tumor came back.

I reminded her, "You remember that I prayed to remove the tumor? So I believe that God heard my prayer, and there is no tumor. Are you having any pain?"

She said, "No pain, but discomfort."

I said, "Go to the doctor and tell him that some dead skin is hanging there. Tell him to take it out."

The doctor checked her and found that there was a dried-up tumor there. He removed it, and there was no pain or blood. When you pray, believe that God heard your prayer. Even though some people try to confuse you, hold onto your faith. Our God is a prayer-answering God.

One full gospel pastor invited me to preach and pray for sick people. After the service, many people lined up for healing. The last person in line was the pastor's wife. I thought she might be guiding people to enter the line, but when I asked her, she said that she needed prayer. I told her to come to the stage, but she said, "No, I have to humble myself and come as everyone else is coming."

When the time came to pray for her, I asked her, "Sister, what can I do for you?"

She said, "I have a tumor the size of a grapefruit. I am scheduled for surgery tomorrow."

I said, "I am going to pray for you, and God is going to make your tumor disappear."

I laid hands on her stomach and prayed in the name of Jesus for her tumor to be healed. After prayer, I asked her to check and see if she had any pain. She felt her stomach everywhere and could not find any pain.

I said, "Thank God that your tumor is gone. You don't have to go for surgery tomorrow. God already did a miracle surgery for you."

She said, "I am scheduled for surgery, and so I have to go."

I said, "It's up to you, but they are not going to find a tumor."

They did the surgery and found a small tumor which was the size of a cherry. After the surgery, she called me and was thankful that the tumor disappeared.

One lady came to our church after hearing our radio program. She was pregnant at the time. She had gone for a check-up, and the doctors told her that she had a tumor. If they took the tumor out, the baby would die. She didn't want to lose her baby. I prayed for her and told her that her baby would be fully delivered, and the tumor would disappear. She said, "I'm a Pentecostal believer. I believe that when we pray, God will hear our prayer." I called her on her due date and told her that she should go for delivery. She safely delivered a healthy baby girl with no deformity, and the tumor disappeared. She came to church with the girl several times and testified about what God had done for her. Many people were blessed because of her testimony.

There was a Christian brother who was also an elder of the church. I met him in his village, and he said, "You're preaching about water baptism and the Holy Spirit. We don't believe in baptism by immersion, and I don't want you to talk about baptism here. Get out of this place."

Jesus said in Matthew 10:14, "And whosoever shall not receive you, nor hear your words, when ye depart out of that house or city, shake off the dust of your feet." This word came into my mind, but I said, "Lord, please forgive me. I'm not going to shake the dust off my feet right now. I'm going to give this man one more chance."

After a while, someone came to my church and told me that an elder from that village had been admitted to the hospital. I didn't know who had been admitted, but I went to visit him. When I saw him, I knew that he was the same man who had told me not to come to his village.

I was not angry with him. Instead, I said to him lovingly, "Uncle, what can I do for you?"

He said, "I have a tumor the size of a coconut. I have severe pain and cannot sleep. I feel like I'm a fish out of water. I'm a villager, and I'm afraid of surgery. They already scheduled a surgery for me. Can you pray that God will heal me, so that I don't have to do the surgery?"

I laid my hand on his stomach and prayed that God would remove the tumor in Jesus' name. As soon as I said "Amen," I asked him, "Do you have any pain?"

He said, "I do not have any more pain."

I told him to check it out, and he started pressing himself everywhere. He could not find any pain.

I said, "That means the tumor has disappeared. Tell your doctor to take another X-ray, and you may not need any surgery. I'll come tomorrow to visit you and see what the doctor says."

The next day I came, and this man was rejoicing. He said, "I do not need surgery. I'm going home today. Please forgive me, because I told you not to come to my village. I invite you to come to my house."

Mark 11:22-24 says we have to have faith in God. When you

pray for anything, believe that God heard your prayer, and, at the same time, if you have anything against anyone, forgive them. I think that's what happened. I forgave that man, and God did a miracle.

OUT OF COMA

I got a phone call from a church member. This brother was a strong believer, as well as a well-built, healthy man. I never saw him crying, but when he called, he was crying. He said, "My wife is in the hospital. She is in a coma." Her brother was a pastor, and there were other pastors sitting around and praying for her.

I said, "Give the phone to the nurse, and I will tell her to give the phone to your wife. I will pray over the phone."

He gave the phone to the nurse, and when I talked to the nurse, she said, "No, I cannot give the phone to her. She is in a coma."

I said, "I am her pastor, and I would like to pray for her."

She said, "There are many pastors praying for her."

I said, "Please keep the phone near her ear, and I will pray for her."

Thank God, she kept the phone near his wife's ear. I called his wife by her name, and as soon as she heard my voice, she replied, "Hi, Pastor Peter. How are you doing?"

I said, "Praise God, I am doing very well. How are you doing?"

She came out of her coma, and she came to church and testified.

One day, I was visiting someone in the hospital. The doctor was looking in on her, and so I was told to sit in the waiting room. As I was waiting, one elderly man saw the Bible in my hand.

"Are you a minister?" he asked me. "Could you please come and pray for my wife? She has been in a coma for a long time."

I said, "Surely I will come and pray for her, and God is going to heal her." I had a strong faith and believed that lady would be healed, because I had prayed for many people in comas, and they had come out of their comas. So I had no doubt that she would be healed. I wasn't sure if this man was Russian or Ukrainian, but he said that his wife didn't speak English. I said, "I'm not praying to her. I'm praying to Jesus, and so I don't have to worry about the language."

I prayed for her in the name of Jesus, and when I said "Amen," she opened her eyes. I said, "Praise the Lord," and she lifted up her hand and said, "Praise the Lord." She was completely healed, and she was released from the hospital.

There is nothing impossible with God. If someone is in a coma, don't think that person is not listening to you. Just go to them and talk to them about Jesus. If they listen to the word of God, they will come to the saving knowledge of Jesus Christ, and they will come out of the coma and live for God.

seven

✿

MIRACLES CONTINUED

O ne man wrote me a letter. In that letter, he said, "My wife is very sick. She is at the point of death. As you read this letter, my wife might be dead."

What would you do if you received such a letter? This man did not have a telephone, and I had no other way to contact him. I just raised my hand toward heaven and said, "Lord, you see this letter. This man is writing to me by faith, but at the same time, he says, 'When you read this letter, my wife might be dead.'"

I wrote him a letter with many Bible scriptures about healing, and I sent the letter, expecting a miracle. I later received another letter, written by his wife, in her own handwriting, saying that she had been healed. A few years later, I visited that family, and she gave her testimony. She said that as soon as she read the letter, she was completely healed. There is no distance in prayer. God's presence is everywhere, and there is nothing impossible with God.

One lady called me and said, "My husband is in the hospital. The doctor gave him one and a half hours to live. Could you please come and pray for him?"

This lady used to come to our church, but her husband used to bring her to the church door and leave. When I said, "Come and attend the service," he refused to come in.

"No, I don't want to come," he said.

"Why?" I said.

"I don't want any part of Jesus," he said. "I don't believe in Jesus."

"Do you believe in God?" I asked.

"I believe in a supreme power," he said. "I don't believe in Jesus Christ."

"One day you will," I said.

He never came to church, and now he was dying. The lady said to me, "He has only one and a half hours to live. Could you hurry up?"

I said, "It's impossible for me to come right away, but if you could talk to him and give the phone to him, I will talk to him."

I said to her husband, "When you used to come to our church and I invited you to come in many times, you said, 'I don't want Jesus. I don't believe in Jesus.' But I'm a servant of Jesus Christ. I'm going to pray for you. Jesus will raise you from your deathbed, and you will serve the Lord."

He said, "I'm ready."

Then I prayed for him and led him to Jesus Christ. God healed that man, and he came out of the hospital. He came to church, went on stage and gave his testimony. He gave me a hug and said, "You're my pastor, and Jesus is my Lord."

Can you imagine if somebody tells you that you're going to die within one and a half hours? What are you going to do? You're going to say, "There is no hope. Now I'm going to die." However, when I reminded that man to confess his sins and receive Jesus Christ as his Lord and Savior, God touched him and healed him. God did it for him, and if you have a problem, He can do it for you.

There was one young man who used to play the organ in our church. He had a girlfriend who came to church as well. As soon as he would see her, he would stop playing the organ and would leave the building, and that girl would follow him. This happened a couple of times, and so I asked the man why he would leave the church when the girl came.

He said, "My family and her family arranged a marriage for us when we were very young, maybe when we were four or five years old. Now it is time for us to get married, but I found out that she has very bad asthma."

I heard that some of the girl's relatives were medical doctors. They tried everything medically, but the girl's condition was not improving.

The young man said, "Brother Peter, pray for this girl, and if she gets healed, then I will marry her."

Then I talked to the girl and asked her, "When you come to church and the boy leaves, why do you leave your Bible and songbooks and run after him?"

She said, "We promised each other a long time ago that we were going to marry each other. Now it is time for marriage, and he doesn't want to marry me. I cannot live without him."

So I said to her, "You have to give your life to Jesus Christ. Then, God can heal you."

However, she did not want to hear what I was saying.

One day, I dreamed that she had fallen into a well, and I was trying to rescue her. When I told her about my dream, she did not pay any attention. Then I saw another dream about her. This time, I saw her lying on her bed and wishing to die. She was telling her youngest brother to call me for prayer. I told her about this dream as well, but she did not pay attention to it. However, one day she was very sick and felt she was going to die, and she sent her youngest brother to call me.

When I went there, she said, "I don't want to live. Please pray for me that I will go to heaven."

I said, "What about that man that you want to marry?"

She said, "I don't care about him anymore."

I said, "Then you have room for Jesus Christ to come into your heart."

She was willing to give her heart to God, and so I led her to Christ. I told her, "Since you gave your heart to Jesus Christ and made Him as your Lord and Savior, now I'm going to pray that God should heal you completely." I prayed for her, and I left. Pretty soon, I saw her completely healed. Her beauty came back to her. She had long hair and a healthy body, and she looked so beautiful. Later on, I heard that the same man asked her to marry him, and that they were happily married.

Medically, it was impossible, but God made it possible. There is nothing impossible with God.

There was a prayer meeting in one farmer's house. After the service, I told the people that, if anyone needed prayer, I would pray for their healing. There was a young lady who was married to the farmer's youngest son. She said, "My sister is very sick. She has been suffering for eight years. They did all kinds of medicine, but she is not getting better. Her husband told her that he could not take care of her and that she should go to her parents' house. Will you be able to come and pray for my sister?"

I went with her to the house. I went inside and said to the lady, "Where is your sister?"

She said to me, "She is lying here on the bed."

I said to her, "I don't see anyone."

She pulled back the bedsheet, and there was her sister. She was so thin that I hadn't noticed her.

I said to this sister, "God is going to heal you right now. Do you have any pain right now, so that I could pray for you?"

She said, "My tooth is aching so much. I cannot bear this pain."

I touched her face and prayed in the name of Jesus to take away her pain. Instantly, the pain was gone. I said to her, "The same Jesus who took your pain away is going to heal your sickness and disease, and you will be completely healed by the power of God. I will be back."

Three months later, I went to see how that girl was doing. There was a young girl sitting outside the house, washing the dishes under a tree.

I asked her, "Last time, I came and prayed for one sister. How is she doing?"

She said, "That's me." She was completely healthy. Her husband got the news, and he came to pick her up. Her husband was sitting in the porch.

She said, "Thank God that you came to see me today, because today I'm going back home with my husband."

Thank God that an incurable disease was healed.

At midnight on Christmas Eve, a Hindu man, twenty-two years old, came knocking at my door. I asked him, "Why did you come here in the middle of the night?"

"I'm a Hindu, and our people do not want us to go to any Christian church. So I came in the middle of the night, so that no one will see me coming here," he said. "I have a blood disease, and the doctors say there is no cure for it. I went to all of my Hindu temples, but no Hindu priest or god did anything for me. One of your church members told me to come to you for prayer."

I said, "You came to the right place. Jesus is the healer. He will heal you completely, if you give your heart to Jesus Christ and ask Jesus to forgive your sins."

I prayed for him in the name of Jesus, and he gave his heart to the Lord. When he went for a check-up the next day, the doctors could not find any trace of disease. He came to the Sunday service and testified that he was completely healed. He was baptized and filled with the Holy Spirit, and he started preaching the word of God. Somebody told me, "I saw that Hindu man who was healed, and he was preaching just like you." I was so thankful to God.

We had an outdoor convention, and we needed some mats. There was a Hindu merchant selling those mats, and I bought so many of them. I gave the merchant my card and invited him to attend the convention.

He said, "I'm a communist party leader. I don't believe in any God."

I said, "Keep this card, and it will come in handy someday," but he threw the card on the ground.

Three years later, he came to my church. "Do you remember me?" he asked.

"I don't remember you," I said.

Then he reminded me that I had bought the mats from him and given him my card, but he had thrown it on the ground. "You told me that someday it would be useful," he said.

Then I remembered him, but when I had seen him the first time, he was a very healthy man. I wasn't able to recognize him now, because he looked very sick.

"I gave up my religion when I became a communist party leader," he said. "But when I became sick, I went to all of my Hindu gods, and they were not able to heal me. Do you think Jesus can heal me?"

"You came to the right place," I said. "What is your sickness?"

"Since three years, I cannot sleep," he said. "Doctors could not help me. I went to Hindu gods, and they could not help me."

I said, "Our God is a miracle-working God, and you will be completely healed. Receive Jesus Christ as your Lord and Savior, confess all your sins to Him, and He will heal you right away."

I laid my hand on his head, prayed in the name of Jesus, and asked God to give him peace and a good night's sleep. He went home rejoicing and came to church for the Sunday service. He looked healthy now.

"I was asleep for the whole week," he said.

"You weren't able to sleep for three years, and so you are refreshed now," I said. "Go for a regular check-up, and see if you are okay."

By the grace of God, he had no problem and was completely healed by the power of God.

One day, I told him that I was going to visit some people in the hospital.

"I'll go with you," he said.

As we were walking through the hospital, one of the doctors said to him, "Hey, you are a communist party leader, and this man is a minister. How can you become friends?"

"If there is a God," he replied, "there is only one God, and that God is Jesus Christ."

I was visiting a Christian brother, and he said, "There is an old lady who is very religious and God-fearing. She loves the servants of God. She is very lonely. You should visit her."

When I went to her house, the door was open, and she was sitting on the floor with an open Bible in her lap. It was a dark room with no light.

I asked, "Mother, are you reading the Bible in this dark?"

She said, "I used to read my Bible every day. Now I am very old and cannot see anything."

I said, "Would you like to read your Bible again? God can open your eyes right now."

I put my thumbs on her eyes and asked God to open her eyes so that she could read the Bible again. As soon as I finished my prayer in the name of Jesus, I asked her if she could see now.

She said, "I can see your face. I can see very well now."

I said, "Now you can read your Bible," and she started reading.

There is nothing impossible with God. Matthew 18:19 says that if two people agree on earth and pray, God will hear their prayer. According to that, it happened exactly. All glory goes to God.

One day, I was shopping at the supermarket, and there was a lady ahead of me at the counter. I had a few items, and she looked at me and said, "Would you like to go ahead of me?"

I thanked her and gave her my card. "I'm a minister," I said.

"If you have any need, please call me, and I will be able to pray for you and your family."

She called me for prayer that night from the hospital. She said, "My husband is very sick. I don't know where he kept all our important papers, because he handles everything. Could you please pray for him so at least he could talk to me and I would know where the papers are?"

So I prayed for him for his healing. God healed that man, and he went home.

About a couple of years later, I received a phone call at midnight from that lady. She said, "Do you remember me? You gave me your card in the supermarket. You prayed for my husband, and God healed him."

I said, "Praise the Lord. What took you so long to call me, and why are you calling me after two years in the middle of the night? What happened?"

She said, "You know, we had a good time. We were going on trips here and there. We got so busy and forgot to call you, but my husband just died."

I said, "I'm sorry to hear that."

She was thankful to God, however. "I wanted one more week with him, but God gave me two more years," she said. "He said to me, 'The man who prayed for me is the only one who can perform my funeral.'"

They had a big church, and it would have been no problem for them to conduct the funeral. However, this man was so thankful that I prayed for him, and I fulfilled his wish. When a person becomes a child of God, we are all brothers and sisters in the Lord, and it is our duty to help one another.

A woman who listened to my radio program called for prayer. In those days, some people did not have phones in their houses, and there were no cell phones at all. However, there were public phones, and if you put in a quarter, the telephone company would give you a limited time to talk. This lady said to me, "I only have one quarter. Please hurry up and pray for me, before my quarter finishes."

I said, "Sister, I am not the healer. Jesus is the healer." I started talking about Jesus and His miracles. After a while, I knew that her time was going to run out, and so I asked her, "What is your prayer request?"

She said, "Now you don't have to pray because I am healed. I have no pain, and I'm completely healed. God healed me."

"Who healed you?" I said.

She said, "The word of God has power. As you were saying some of the word of God, I got touched, and I got healed."

I told her, "You can come to our church and testify." She came with her whole family, and she testified about what Jesus Christ had done for her.

When we pray for someone, we should not be taking credit that we healed someone. The word of God has power to heal. Jesus Christ is the word of God, and Jesus is the healer. All glory goes to Jesus Christ.

I was invited to one full gospel church. After the service, I prayed for so many people. As I was ready to leave, one grandmother came to me and said, "Could you come and pray for my granddaughter?"

I wondered why she didn't bring her granddaughter to pray during the service. The girl might have been eight years old. She looked very depressed and weak. I did not ask the grandmother what kind of sickness or disease the child had. I just laid hands on the child and prayed that God would heal her completely. "God heard my prayer," I said to the grandmother, "and your granddaughter is healed."

She never called me, and I didn't hear anything from her. A year later, the pastor of the same church invited me again. After the service, this grandmother came to me and said, "Do you remember praying for my granddaughter?"

I said, "How is she doing?"

She said, "I didn't tell you what was the problem, but I'm telling you now. She had brain damage." She didn't tell me how it happened. "After you prayed, God healed her completely. She is in school now, and she has good grades."

Even though I didn't know what the girl's problem was, Jesus knew. However, any healing would not come automatically. Someone has to ask for healing, because the glory has to go to God. Matthew 7:7 says, "Ask, and it shall be given to you," and that word is true. When you ask by faith, God answers prayer. Matthew 18:19 says that if two people agree touching anything, God will hear our prayer from heaven. That is what happened in this situation. Again I say, we are not the healer. Jesus is the healer, and the glory goes to Him.

One lady used to work in a very famous diner. Her husband was a teacher working at a Bible college. Somehow, he died in his fifties. This lady came to our church, and I baptized her. She started coming regularly to our church. She saw many healings and miracles in our church.

One day, she said to her manager, "Your father has throat cancer. I can tell Pastor Peter to pray for him, and God can heal him."

The manager and his father were Catholic, but the manager said to her, "If you could, please tell your pastor to go to the hospital and pray for my father there."

When I went there, her manager's father said to me, "I wanted to be a priest, but I did not become one. That is why God is mad at me, and he gave me cancer to punish me."

I said, "Sir, you got it wrong. The Bible says the enemy comes to steal, kill and destroy. That enemy is the devil. Jesus said, 'I am come that they might have life, and that they might have it more abundantly' (John 10:10). Our God is loving and kind. He never gives anyone sickness or disease. The devil is lying to you and telling you that God gave you this disease, so that you will hate God." I gave him a short message about salvation, and I told him,

"Jesus is the healer. I'm going to pray for you, and God is going to heal you right now."

He was very grateful that I prayed for him, and I left.

The next morning, his son called me and said, "My father is very upset."

I said, "Why is your father upset?"

He said, "After you left, the doctor gave him a very bad report, that the cancer has spread throughout his body."

I said, "Sir, that report was done before I prayed. I prayed, and God heard my prayer. Please take him for a check-up. You will have a good check-up, and there will be no trace of cancer in his body." He went for a check-up, and the doctors could not find a trace of cancer.

It was the month of February, and the snow was up to my knees, when he came and knocked at my door.

I could not recognize him, and so I said, "Sir, what can I do for you?"

He said, "Do you remember that you came to the hospital and prayed for me? I had throat cancer, but I want to tell you that I am completely cured. There is no trace of cancer in my body. I just wanted to come in person and tell you the good news."

I said to him, "You didn't have to come in this kind of weather."

He said, "I am so grateful to God and grateful to you. I just had to come in person and thank you."

I thank God that, even though the enemy gave him bad news, Jesus gave him good news. Our God is a good God.

There was a Christian brother. He used to go to a Baptist church for twenty years, but somehow he stopped going to that church. He started visiting many churches, and he became disappointed. He thought to himself, "I am a born again child of God. I have twenty years of experience with Christianity. I'm not going to go to any church. I'm going to start my own Bible bookstore." He was very happy with his Bible bookstore.

He had a friend who used to help him with his store. This man was very talented. He could fix any electronic machines, and he was also a pilot. Somehow, he felt some weakness in his body and could not work for more than three hours. When he asked me for prayer, I prayed for him. I gave him some electrical work to do at the church. He worked for almost twelve hours without rest. He was very happy and started coming regularly to our church.

He told his friend who ran the bookstore to come to our church. However, the man who ran the bookstore said, "All the churches are the same. I'm not going to go to any church. If you like that church, you go to that church."

We were putting in a new heating system. I was talking to the mechanic about Christ, and he was very interested to listen. He said that he was a believer, and he and his family attended church services outside the state. They started attending our church regularly.

One day, this mechanic was sent to repair the bookstore owner's heating system. He started telling the bookstore owner about our church. The bookstore owner said, "Two people cannot be wrong." He decided to visit our church, and he liked it.

He gave me a prayer request. There was fluid inside his elbow, and it was hanging about six inches. Someone told him to go to the hospital, but he said, "No, I want Pastor Peter to pray for me." I prayed for him, and after the service he came to show me that the fluid disappeared. However, the hanging skin had hardened, and he asked me to pray for the hardened skin to disappear. I prayed again, and the following Sunday he came to church, rolled up his sleeve and said, "My elbow is completely healed, just like the other elbow." He started glorifying God, and his faith increased.

One evangelist arranged a meeting in a big church and invited me to preach there. The pastor of that church had been ministering there for fifty years. I spent the day visiting the neighborhood, and I started the service at 6:00 in the evening. I asked people to come to the altar if they had any need, any sickness or disease, so that

I could pray for them, and people were lined up until 5:00 in the morning. Many miracles happened.

The pastor of the church was very happy and started crying. He said, "I am serving the Lord for this many years, but I never saw miracles like this. It seems like what was written in the book of Acts is happening today."

I knew that this church didn't believe in the holy communion or baptism by immersion, but I started thinking that all of these people who got saved and healed should be baptized. I asked the pastor for permission to baptize them, and he was very glad. He said, "Even if I lose my job, I don't care. God's will should be done."

I was very thankful, and I prayed that God would provide the water to baptize all of these people. I was surprised to find that there was a pond behind the church. There was plenty of water, and I was able to baptize the people who were ready to be baptized.

There is nothing impossible with the Lord. The word of God says in Acts 16:31 that if you believe in the Lord, you will be saved and your household. However, your household is not going to be saved automatically; they have to come to Jesus. They have to receive Jesus Christ as their Lord and Savior. You have to tell them, because the word of God says that faith comes by hearing, and hearing by the word of God. What is your need? Are you sick or afflicted? Are you having problems in your family? Whatever your problem is, call upon Jesus. Jesus is the answer. There is nothing impossible with God.

eight

✿

GOD FULFILLED HIS PROMISE

G od told me that He would take me to America, and that
promise was fulfilled.

JOURNEY TO USA

When God called me for the ministry, I was faithfully serving
the Lord in my hometown. From there, I traveled all over India.
Then I came to Gujarat from Bombay and served the Lord there
for almost ten years. In the beginning, I had only a bicycle. I used
the bicycle to go to surrounding areas and preach the gospel,
going to several places. Later on, God gave me a car. At that time
in India, not many people had a car. Only rich people and some
professionals would have cars, but very few ministers had cars at
that time. I was so grateful to God when I got my car, and I started
visiting several places by car.

At that time, by the grace of God, I had everything that I
needed for evangelistic work. I used to print and distribute my
own literature. Other ministries also sent us their literature, and
so we were distributing literature everywhere. We had our own

public address system which we used outdoors. We were doing all kinds of services, in different halls, indoors and outdoors. Our church was the fastest growing church in that area. I was very happy with my ministry, and I never thought about leaving that area and going someplace else.

As I was reading my Bible, I came to Acts 1:8: "But ye shall receive power, after that the Holy Ghost is come upon you: and ye shall be witnesses unto me both in Jerusalem, and in all Judea, and in Samaria, and unto the uttermost part of the earth."

I started thinking. I preached the gospel all over India. I even wanted to go to Pakistan and preach the gospel, but they did not give me a visa, because there was a war between India and Pakistan at the time. So when I read this scripture, I said, "Lord, how can I fulfill this scripture, going to the uttermost part of the world?"

Then God spoke to me in my spirit that he would take me to America and, from there, I would be able to preach the gospel around the world.

I did not fully understand how this was going to work, but I believed in my heart. At that time, I did not speak English. I did not have money in the bank. Whatever money I was getting, I was using for evangelistic work. So I did not have any bank balance. I was thinking that it was humanly impossible for me to go, but if God wanted me to go, I trusted that He would make a way for me.

So I put my faith in action and started working on it. I told everyone that I wanted to go to the USA. I applied for my passport. It was so difficult to get a passport at the time. The passport office told me that I had to have twenty thousand rupees in my bank account, or else that someone would have to sponsor me and guarantee me for twenty thousand dollars. By the grace of God, I had rich church members. If I had asked any one of them, they would have sponsored me, but I never asked anyone. I kept on praying.

One lady visited our church a couple of times and gave me a

couple of prayer requests. God answered her prayers, and she and her husband were so grateful.

"I heard you are going to the USA," she said. "Is there anything we can do for you?"

"I'm waiting for my passport," I said. "The passport office said I needed twenty thousand rupees, or else someone has to sponsor me."

Her husband said to me, "We will be more than happy to help you," and both of them agreed. "I have money in three different banks," he continued. "I'll give you a bankbook and a letter, and the bank will give you a sponsorship letter."

By the grace of God, I got the letter, submitted it to the passport office, and got my passport. After I got my passport, I was praying to God that I would get my visa. Getting a visa was more difficult than getting a passport in those days. Only businesspeople who wanted to do business in America or professionals like doctors, nurses, lawyers, and engineers would get visas to go to America, or else someone from America would need to sponsor you. I had no such qualifications.

Then I thought to myself that I could ask ministers in America to sponsor me. I wrote to Billy Graham, T. L. Osborn, and Oral Roberts. I didn't get a favorable response from Billy Graham, but T. L. Osborn said that he was willing to sponsor me to work in London. I didn't know anything about London, and I wondered if London and America were the same. I said to myself that, if God wanted me to go to America, I wasn't going to London.

However, I was much encouraged by the letter that I received from Oral Roberts. He wrote that the steps of a good man are ordered by the Lord (Psalm 37:23). I started thanking God and said, "I am the righteousness of God. Jesus Christ shed His precious blood for me and washed away my sins. In the sight of God, I am righteous. So God is going to order my steps, and I will be in the USA."

The daughter of one of my Christian friends was going to

America. Before she left, she asked me to sing some songs and make a tape recording, which she took to America. I started telling people, "You know what? My voice is in the USA. That means someday I will be going to the USA." However, I never thought in my heart to ask her to sponsor me. I was just praying that God would open a door for me someday.

By the grace of God, I got married to a nurse three days before she left for America to study nursing at New York University. She also started working at a hospital in New York, and so she was able to sponsor me from the USA. She sent me several sponsor letters, but since I was traveling in different parts of India at the time, I did not get several of the letters. Finally, the fifth time that she sent me the sponsorship letter and forms, I received them.

I went to the visa office to get my visa. There was a lady checking my sponsorship letter at the counter. Looking at the paper, she said, "This is not good enough. The person who is sponsoring you should have five to ten thousand dollars in their bank account. I need proof from an American bank that there is enough money to support you. Until you have this proof, please don't come here again."

I left without saying a word and went back home. That night, a Christian pastor came to see me. When I told him that my sponsorship letter had been rejected, he started comforting me. "You have a good ministry here," he said. "You don't have to go to America."

Another pastor who had a church with five thousand members told me that he was going to retire, and he wanted to hand the church over to me. I would have gotten five thousand rupees per week, but I said to him, "I am not going to the USA to make money, and I'm not going to take over somebody's church."

That night, I prayed, "Lord, I went there, and they rejected my paper. What should I do now?"

I felt in my spirit that, although I had gone there already, I would go again the next day by faith. I believed that God would give me my visa.

Early in the morning, I started my journey, because it was a long journey. I arrived at the visa office before it opened and stood in line outside. When I went inside, I saw the same lady standing at the counter. There was one person standing in front of me, and she took his paper. As she looked at his paper, I prayed, "Lord, please move her away from here, or else she will give me a hard time." She took his paper and went into the back of the office, and another gentleman came. When my number came, he called me and looked at my sponsorship letter.

"Is this paper okay for my sponsorship letter?" I asked him.

"It looks fine," he said.

"When will I get my visa?" I asked.

"It will take a couple of days," he said.

"Can I get it today?" I said.

"You have to go to two different doctors, and it takes time," he said. "But you will get it."

"If I get both of the doctor's reports today, can I get it?" I asked.

"If you can get it, come before 3:30," he said, "because at 3:30 we close."

"Could you please sign that these papers are okay and seal it, so that nobody will bother me when I come?" I asked.

He signed them and said, "Come before 3:30, and you will get your visa."

I thanked him and walked away. As I was leaving, my travel agent said to me, "Mr. Peter, the man who was checking your paper, do you know who that person was? That man was the consulate general. He is in charge of this whole department, and you were talking to him as if he was an ordinary clerk. Once he checked your paper and said it was okay, no one has authority to cancel it."

I thanked God and went hurriedly to do my doctor's check-ups.

First, I went to have my X-rays taken. By the grace of God, they took my X-rays and gave them to me right away. I was so happy, and I rushed to the next medical department. When I went there, I saw one Gujarati man sitting there and looking very depressed.

I asked him, "How are you, and what kind of business do you do?"

He said, "I have an accounting firm, and I want to go to the USA to expand my business. But I am having a problem getting my medical report. I have been failing every time, for six months."

I said, "I am a servant of God. I am going to pray for you, and this time you are going to pass." Pretty soon, his report came, and he passed. He was very happy.

"See you in the USA," I said.

"I'll wait here until your report comes," he said.

"Don't worry," I said. "I'll pass the first time."

My report came, and I passed my test. They asked me to pay a fee to release the report. I looked in my wallet, and I didn't have the money.

"I'll go home and bring the money," I said, but that would have been a six-hour journey.

The man for whom I had prayed was still there. "You don't have to go home. I'll pay the money," he said, and he paid the fee for my report.

I rushed back to the visa office before 3:30 and submitted those papers. After a few minutes, I asked the clerk, "When am I going to get my visa?"

He pointed to a basket, and inside was my passport, with my visa attached inside.

I thanked God, and I went home very excited. The next day, I went to that accountant's house and repaid him the money that he had given me to pay for my medical check-up. I took my passport and visa and returned to my headquarters in Gujarat. Now I was praying for a ticket for airfare to travel to the USA. I did not ask anyone if they could help me.

One day, I was visiting an evangelist, and he told me that I should go with him to pray for him in a different city. When I went there, I realized that my travel agent's office was there. I was tempted to go to the office and ask about the ticket, but I didn't, because I didn't have the money to purchase a ticket at that time. To my surprise, someone came and gave me an envelope, and I saw that it was from the travel agent. I had not contacted him, and it's a miracle that he wrote to me.

"Let's open it and see what's inside," said the evangelist.

"I don't want to open it here, in case he is asking for money," I said.

We went back to the evangelist's home, and then I laid my hand on the envelope and prayed that there should be a ticket inside. When I opened the envelope, I found a ticket with my name and the traveling route correctly printed on it. However, there was no letter from him asking for money for the ticket. So I thanked God and traveled back to Bombay.

I told my parents and my brothers that I was going to the USA, and they came to the airport with me to say goodbye. At that time, the Indian government only allowed me to take ten dollars with me. I said goodbye to everyone, gave them the rest of my money, and went to board the plane.

Before I boarded the plane, I was told to pay an airport tax. I didn't know anything about it. The man standing behind me in line offered to pay for me. I thanked him and told him that I would pay him back. He gave me the address of his destination in Canada, and I got on the plane.

I arrived at the airport in New York, paid ten dollars to the taxi driver and went to Brooklyn. I made sure to pay back the man who was in Canada. I received a beautiful letter from my travel agent. He congratulated me on my arrival in America. He asked me if I would give twenty-five dollars a month to his brother, who was studying at New York University, as pocket money. It was easy for me, and I also paid back the ticket money. I was thankful to God that he didn't ask for the money when I was in India.

Afterward, God opened the door for me to go to Philadelphia, Pennsylvania.

MY FIRST CHURCH IN AMERICA

By the grace of God, I came to America in 1969. I was in New York, and I was planning to go to Philadelphia. People started telling me not to go because Philadelphia was not a good city. They said that Philadelphia had a lot of crime. I said, "That's the place I want to go and preach the gospel."

Philippians 2:15 says, "That ye may be blameless and harmless, the sons of God without rebuke, in the midst of a crooked and perverse nation, among whom ye shine as lights in the world." When I was in India, God used me in parts of India that were worse than Philadelphia. That's why I was not afraid to come to Philadelphia. God opened the door for me to come to Philadelphia, and so I believed that God would protect me in Philadelphia.

When I came to Philadelphia, I prayed about starting a church in the USA. I didn't know anyone in Philadelphia. I started visiting local churches and testifying about what God had done in my life. By the grace of God, I made many friends. I met one godly pastor, and I asked him for advice about how to start a church in Philadelphia. At that time, there were three or four large churches in Philadelphia. All of them were registered by the same lawyer. The pastor took me to see that lawyer, and he helped me to register our church. That pastor helped me every step of the way, and by the grace of God, our church was registered in 1971. However, we still didn't have a church building. I was visiting other churches and giving my testimony, and many churches gave me a chance to preach.

One day I saw one beautiful church building in the middle of a residential area. I wasn't sure whether this was a church building, because there was no sign in front. So I waited there, praying in my spirit, and a man came outside to do cement work on the front steps.

I asked him, "Is this a church?"

He said, "Yes."

I said, "What kind of church?"

He said, "This is a Ukrainian Pentecostal full gospel church."

I was very happy to know that this was a full gospel church. I said, "Can I use this church for our services?"

He said, "Well, I am just the deacon, but if you come to church Sunday, we can talk to the church board. If they like you, they might approve, and you might use this church."

So I was excited. I told some of the people who were coming to our house to pray on Sunday, "I am going to go. You people pray, and today we will have some good news."

I talked to the pastor and the church board. I gave them my testimony, and they liked me so much that they said that I could use their building.

I said, "How much do I have to pay?"

They said, "Oh, you don't have to pay anything."

I said, "No, I have to pay something."

So they said, "Give us fifty dollars per month."

I was so happy, and we started our service there the following Sunday.

People from the neighborhood started coming to our church, even though we didn't have a church sign or telephone. Pretty soon, we started our first radio program. That program was reaching Philadelphia, Delaware, and New Jersey. All kinds of people started coming.

However, someone came and said to me, "You cannot invite all kinds of people to this neighborhood."

I said to him, "John 3:16 says, 'For God so loved the world that He gave His only begotten Son, that whosoever believeth in Him should not perish but have everlasting life.' So, if God loves the whole world, why can't we love the whole world?"

He didn't answer me, and he walked away.

Soon after that, on the first Sunday of the month, someone set fire to the building. The fire station was half a block from there, and I was surprised that they were not able to save the church.

One pastor from a nearby Methodist church said that we could use their basement for our services, and I thanked him for the offer. There was another pastor there who had a Portuguese Pentecostal church. I knew him very well, because he had come to our church many times. He said that we could use his church. I asked him how much I would have to pay, and he said one hundred dollars per month. It was twice as much as I had been paying before, but the location was very good. It was a couple of miles away, near a highway and easily accessible to public transportation. It had a parking lot with a fence and plenty of street parking. I was very happy for his offer, and we started our service the same day.

We started a radio program that aired five days a week, and more people started coming. The church was almost full, and the parking lot was full. The owner of the building was a different person, a Baptist pastor. He came to me and said, "Your church is growing so fast, and we cannot accommodate you. You can go somewhere and find your own building."

I didn't have the money, because I was using the church money for the radio broadcasts. I didn't know where to go. It was February. There was snow on the ground, and it was bitterly cold. I said, "Could you wait until April, so we can go to the park and preach the gospel there?"

He said, "No, that's your problem. You have to find somewhere."

I felt sad that a Christian pastor didn't understand our situation. He told the Portuguese pastor to leave as well, but I was the first to go. The Portuguese pastor had the money to buy his own building and start his own church.

I was searching for a church building, and I saw a large, beautiful building that belonged to the Salvation Army. I went inside and asked the pastor, "Is it possible to use your church building for our services?"

"No one asked me to rent our building. You are the first one to ask," he said. He asked me for four times more than the other church had been asking.

I said, "Can you reduce the rent?"

He said, "No. If God wants you to use our facility, then God will provide."

I agreed and said, "We will start our service this Sunday."

Then he said to me, "You have a choice. You can use our sanctuary for your services, or you can use the basement."

I said, "Sir, you are the owner of the building. You should be using the sanctuary. We will use the basement."

Once I gave him the word, I started praying about how to pay the rent. I decided to terminate all of my radio programs, and we started our services in the basement. Slowly, we started growing, and then we started our radio program again (but this time it was a weekly program, not five days a week). The church had a parking lot, and so the radio listeners had no trouble with parking.

One day, the pastor of the Salvation Army church said to me, "Can we have a combined service for Good Friday?"

I said, "Our church is a full gospel church. We take communion every Sunday, and we will especially take it on Good Friday. Your church does not take communion. Do you think that it will be a problem if your church members take communion with us?"

He said, "It's no problem."

So we had a combined service on Good Friday. Many of the Salvation Army members took communion for the first time, and they were very happy. We took some prayer requests and prayed for people as well.

To my surprise, on Easter Sunday, the pastor came to me and told me to vacate the church. I didn't ask him why, but I told him that it was short notice and asked for some time to find a new building. However, his church members started saying, "Pastor

Peter is praying for us. Their church is not doing any harm to us. Why do we have to let them go?" Pretty soon, I heard that this man was transferred to somewhere else. Then another pastor came, and the same thing happened. He was transferred to another place, and a third pastor came.

He asked me, "Do you have any written contract with us?"

I said, "No, sir."

Then he said, "That means we can tell you to leave at any time, and you will go?"

I said, "Yes, sir."

This pastor gave permission for children to play basketball on top of the room we were using, and so we had a lot of disturbance and noises.

I complained to him, and he said, "Well, these young people are doing it. I cannot tell them not to do it."

I said, "There is a playground, as well as the parking lot. Why do they have to do it inside and make noise while we are praying?"

However, he did not stop them. He wanted to make us miserable so that we would leave.

Young people used to come to the basement and dance there on Saturday night. When we came there on Sunday, the podium and chairs were in disarray. We had to re-arrange everything, and I complained to the pastor again. I said, "Could you at least tell them, while they're leaving, to arrange the chairs properly? Because when we come to set up everything, it takes our time."

He said, "Well, you know, young people these days, we can't tell them what to do."

Then one day, when I came to the basement, I smelled rose petals and incense, and it reminded me of Hindu worship. So I asked the pastor, "What is this smell?"

He said, "We gave the basement to the Hindu people for Hindu worship."

As I was writing this, my son said to me, "Why didn't you take the sanctuary in the first place when they offered it to you, especially with all the money they were charging you? You wouldn't have had to deal with all these activities in the basement if you were in the sanctuary, where the church services were usually held."

Well, it's too late to do anything about it now.

At this point, I decided that it was time to move, and so I prayed that we would find a new building. By the grace of God, I found a bicycle shop, which we remodeled. Many people started coming, and there was not enough parking.

I said, "Lord, You have to give us a building with a parking lot." We saw one building, near the bus and train terminals. This was a single building with a parking lot, and we wanted to buy that building. The real estate people said that you had to place a deposit, and so we placed $10,000.

The following Sunday, one of our church members stood up and said, "We don't have to move from here. We are not agreeing to buying another building."

However, we had already paid the money for the deposit, and I didn't know what to do. I started praying, "Lord, if this building is not for us, I need my money back, but if I ask the real estate agency to give me my money back, they are not going to give it to me."

One day, the real estate agent called and said, "Dr. Peter, in our company we have other agents working on the same building. They have found another customer, and that customer is paying more than what you agreed. So if you want to match the price or give a little bit more than him, then we can give it to you."

I said, "No, sir, you agreed to this price, whatever the price was, and we cannot change that in the middle of the way. So if you want to make more money, you can sell it to somebody. You can give my deposit back."

He said, "No problem. Come to my office, and I'll give you a check," and I got my money back right away.

So we thought, "Now we are going to stay until God opens the new door." Meanwhile, the person who was opposed to buying a new building left our church, and about thirty people left with him.

One day, I saw another building, much better than the other building. This was a corner building with a parking lot, and I liked it very much. I called the real estate agent and said, "I'm interested in this building. Could you send me the information about this building?"

The real estate agent said, "This building is $950,000."

I waited for three weeks, but he did not send me any information. So I had three weeks to pray about it.

The real estate agent called and said, "Dr. Peter, you might be wondering why I did not reply you. I already sent you a letter. In that letter, you will find that I reduced the original price by $200,000. The building price is now $750,000."

"Thank you," I said.

I went to the post office to pick up the letter, and I was very happy. I called one of our church members and said, "Let's go and see the building."

It was morning, and we were just looking around. There was snow on the ground, and one lady came outside wearing a nightgown and slippers. "Gentlemen," she said, "what are you looking at?"

I said, "We are looking at the building. We are going to buy this building."

She said, "This building is sold."

I said, "How come? I have the paper in my hand. How come this building was sold that fast?"

She said, "You don't believe me?"

I said, "Ma'am, if you can show me who bought the building, then I'll know."

She said, "Follow me."

At the time, it seemed foolish to follow that lady in a nightgown and slippers through the snow, but I followed her and trusted in the Lord.

She took us to another building across the street and said, "Wait here, and the man will come."

We were waiting inside as she went to another room, and she returned with an axe in her hand.

"Are you going to kill us or something?" I said.

"No, no," she said. "I'm taking this to another building."

"Where is the man who purchased the building?" I said.

She said, "He will be here in a few minutes," and so we waited.

Pretty soon, the man came. He asked us, "Gentlemen, are you interested in that building?"

I said, "Yes."

Then he showed us the building, and we liked it very much.

Then he said, "This building is not for sale."

I said, "Why did you show us the building, if it is not for sale?"

He said, "I bought this building, but this building is for rent. I have two customers. They are doctors, chiropractors, and they are going to give me $6,500 per month. If you can give me the same amount, I will rent the building to you instead, because you are a servant of God and I like you."

I said, "We are not interested in renting. We are interested in buying."

He said, "Come to my office."

We went to his office, and I said, "Let's pray." I prayed, "Lord, we want this building for your glory. We want to start a church in this neighborhood. Please touch this man's heart. When his heart changes, he will sell us this building. So please change his heart, in Jesus' name. Amen."

When I finished the prayer, the man looked at me and said, "God already changed my heart."

"What do you mean?" I said.

"I decided to sell it to you," he said.

"Praise God," I said. "Prayer works."

The prior real estate agent was going to sell the building for $750,000, but this agent bought the building for $550,000. "Since you're a man of God, and I like you, I'm going to sell it for the same price that I bought it, $550,000. My commission will be $50,000, but that will be separate," he said. "I will make the paperwork for $550,000, and the $50,000 you can give me little by little."

"Okay," I said.

I applied to several banks for a mortgage, but it was very difficult to get a mortgage for a church. At the same time, the interest rates were very high. This new real estate agent said to me, "Dr. Peter, I'm going to introduce you to a friend who is a banker."

He invited the banker to his office, and I talked with him. I told him why we wanted the building, how God blessed me, and why I came to America. I told him that this would be our headquarters and that we were going to preach the gospel around the world. I told him all of these things, and he was very impressed. He did not ask me any financial questions. Instead, he stood up and said, "Let me shake your hand," and I shook his hand.

"You got the mortgage," he said.

I said, "How much is the application fee and all other expenses?"

"Don't worry about that," he said. "We'll take care of it. My word is like pure gold."

I trusted his word, and by the grace of God, we got the mortgage.

We were going for the settlement, and I said to the real estate agent, "You know, on the side of the building, there are so many bushes, and it doesn't look good. Can we trim them down, or cut them down?"

"I'll do it after the settlement," he said.

"Nobody does it after the settlement," I said. "Can you do it now before we go?"

"Okay," he said.

The real estate man called a couple of people. They came with a chainsaw, cut down the bushes, and put everything in front of the building. Then he said, "Dr. Peter, now pray and ask God to bring an empty dump truck, so we can throw this in the trash."

I prayed, and I said, "God will send the empty truck."

By the grace of God, an empty truck came by. The real estate agent stopped the truck and asked the people in the truck to help us pick up the trash. We dumped everything in the truck.

The real estate man said, "You know what? God listens to your prayers."

I said, "Yes, sir. Our God is a prayer-answering God."

We went for the settlement that same day. By the grace of God, we got the building. It was impossible, but God made it possible.

Since then, we have been using this building as a church. There were three different companies using this building, a printer, a real estate agent, and an insurance agent, and so we had to remodel it into a hall. After the settlement, the real estate agent helped a lot with cutting the grass, removing the snow, bringing food and drink for people working on the church and more.

In front of our church, there is a sign, "International Christian Fellowship." On the side, there is another sign that says, "International Christian Fellowship World Outreach Center." By the grace of God, we started spreading the gospel around the world through the internet, print, radio, and television.

What God promised me in India, that is fulfilled. We are in this building, preaching the word of God throughout the world and waiting for Christ to come, and as long as Christ keeps me alive, I promise God that I'm going to serve the Lord, as long as I'm able to preach.

nine

ﻌﻌ

VICTORY OVER THE EYE PROBLEM

I was having difficulty with my vision, but I didn't pay any attention. Eventually, my right eye was completely blind, but I had some vision in my left eye. So I managed to drive and do everything.

One day my wife noticed the cataracts in my eyes. She said, "You have a big cataract growing in your right eye."

I said, "Don't worry, it will be all right. Everything will be all right."

"Even if you don't want to get surgery, at least you should try to have your eyes checked and get eyeglasses," she said.

"No, I gave up my eyeglasses, and I don't need any eyeglasses," I said. So I did not listen to her, but God showed me a dream that my wife took me to a doctor and he did something to my eyes. I didn't know if it was surgery or what he had done to my eyes. However, he was standing beside me afterward, and I could see very clearly. I did not tell my wife about my dream, but my eyesight got even worse. I couldn't see well enough to do any paperwork or read properly, and it became difficult to drive and park my car properly.

One day we were going for shopping, and my wife said to me, "Look, here is an eyeglasses store. How about we go and check your eyes to get a pair of glasses?"

We went to make an appointment, but we were told that there would not be an opening for another two weeks.

My wife said, "There is another place nearby. Why don't we go there?"

We went there for a check-up for me to get eyeglasses, and those people almost blinded me, rubbing my eyes, putting medicines in my eyes, and sending me to different machines to be checked. I was so exhausted, and my eyes started hurting even more.

Finally, the lady at the eyeglasses store said, "We cannot give you eyeglasses."

My wife asked her, "What's the problem?"

"He has a very large cataract in his right eye, and his left eye is almost fifty percent bad with cataracts," she replied. "So we cannot give him a prescription for eyeglasses. The eyeglasses are not going to help him at this point anyway." She suggested that I go to an ophthalmologist and have my cataracts removed in order to see.

So we had to go to a primary doctor to get a referral. I went there, and they checked my blood pressure. The blood pressure was very high, and the doctor got so concerned.

"Your blood pressure is too high," she said. "We have to send you to a heart specialist."

I didn't say anything.

Then she said, "You have to go for some blood tests."

We went and did a blood test. When the report came, the doctor called our home and talked with my wife. The doctor said to her, "Listen, your husband's PSA (Prostate Specific Antigen) is very, very high. It is 62.7 [normal is less than 4]. That means he has advanced stage prostate cancer. He has to see a urologist right away, and he has high blood pressure too."

They thought I was dying. The doctor said, "I cannot give you a referral to any eye doctor for right now. The best thing for you to do is to go to a urologist, because your PSA is so high. That means you have cancer growing in your body." The doctor said that she had never seen such a high PSA.

The doctor talked with my wife again and told her that I had advanced cancer, and that I should be concerned about getting treatment for that instead of cataract surgery. The doctor refused to give me a referral to an eye doctor before seeing a urologist, and so they sent me to a urologist.

I told my wife, "Listen. Why am I going there? They are going to say, 'You have cancer, you have this, you have that.' I'm not going to take any medicine or any other treatment for that anyhow."

"But they told you to go," she said. "We'll go, otherwise they will not give you referral for your eye surgery."

I said, "I'm not going to allow them to do anything."

"Then they will not even see you," she said. "They will tell you to go somewhere else."

"I'll take care of it," I said.

I went there, and the doctor sent my wife out of the room. The doctor put on his gloves to examine me, and I said to him, "Listen, you're not going to touch my body. You can only take the urine and test the urine. If I have cancer, it will show in the urine, right?"

I gave them the urine sample, and I waited there. The test result came, and he said, "You have no problem in your urine."

I said, "Can I have my eye surgery?"

He said, "Yeah, you can go and get your eye surgery."

So I said, "Do you know the doctor?"

He said, "Yeah, I know him."

Then he called my wife and said, "You tell the doctor I told him you can do eye surgery, no problem," but he did not give me anything in writing. He said, "Do you want to do another blood test?"

"You can write it down," I said.

So he gave me the paperwork to do another blood test, but I never did. Since he gave an okay to the doctor to do my eye surgery, I never went back to my primary doctor. If I went, she was going to say, "Did you go to the urologist?" If I said, "Well, I didn't do what he wanted to do," she would not give me a referral.

The eye doctor told me, "Hey, I checked your eyes, but your eyes are very, very bad. I cannot see behind your eyes. So I have to do an ultrasound."

"Do whatever you want to do," I said.

The doctor tried to do the ultrasound, but the machine broke. So he said, "You have to go to an ultrasound specialist, and then he will do the ultrasound. Without that, I cannot do surgery."

I said, "Wait a minute. Do you know anyone who can do it that fast?"

He said, "Okay, my secretary will call and make an appointment for you to go for an ultrasound." They called and set the date and everything.

I went home and said to my wife, "I'm not going to go to any other place for doing my ultrasound, because this eye doctor did an ultrasound and it was very painful. It's hurting so much. My surgery is on the thirteenth, and it's almost the seventh. It's already hurting. If I go for a second ultrasound, my eyes will be hurting more." So I said, "I'm not going."

She said, "You have to talk to the doctor, because they're not going to do the surgery."

I said, "Okay. It's my eyes. If they don't do it, I don't have to do it." So my wife called the doctor's office and said, "My husband doesn't want to do another ultrasound."

The nurse said, "The doctor will not do any surgery without doing an ultrasound."

I said, "Ma'am, please tell the doctor to call me. I want to talk to him."

The doctor called me and said, "You have to go for an ultrasound. Otherwise, I cannot do the surgery."

I said, "Sir, wait a minute. When I first came to your office, you saw the cataract, and you said to me, 'It's very bad. I never did surgery on someone with eyes like yours, but I can do it.' At that time, you didn't tell me that you cannot do surgery without the ultrasound. You said, 'I can do it.' Why did you change your word? You said you were going to do it. Don't you know there are many, many eye doctors? You just tell me that you cannot do it. I'll go somewhere else."

"Don't you worry. I promised you I'll do the surgery. I'll do it," he said.

"If I take you to Wills Eye Hospital, with your high blood pressure, they will never allow me to do surgery," he said. "So you have to go to Jeanes Hospital, and they will do the medical testing again. Then, when the report comes, we'll do it."

I prayed, "Lord, I do not want any more blood tests. I do not want them to do any more torture."

I asked my wife, "What are they going to do?"

She said, "Oh, they will put a monitor, they're going to check your heart, they're going to check your blood."

I said, "They are not going to do anything. I'm not going to allow them to do anything!" It sounds foolish, right?

At the hospital, a nurse looked at me and told me to go and see another nurse. Another nurse came and was very nice.

"Praise the Lord," I said.

"I'm a born again Christian," she said.

So I said, "God sent the right person here." I waited as she checked my eyes and blood pressure.

"No more blood tests," she said, "because if you're going for eye surgery, no blood test is required."

"Praise God!" I said.

When I was scheduled for the surgery, so many people came to check me. The anesthesiologist said, "I'm going to give you some anesthesia."

I said, "Okay, do it a little bit less. Don't kill me."

He said, "We're not going to give too much."

When they started the surgery, I had so much pain, but I didn't say anything. I was thinking in my mind, "Jesus Christ was crucified on the cross. I don't think I'm suffering that much pain. He already took my pain on the cross, so I don't have to worry."

They did surgery on my right eye, and after surgery they covered that eye with bandages and tape. The next day was my check-up after surgery. I could not see a thing. I said, "I cannot see anything. I cannot even see the light. I see very dark shadows."

The doctor became very discouraged. "I told you before, I cannot guarantee that you will be able to see with this eye," he said.

"That's not your fault," I said. "I already told you, you do your job, and God will give me the sight. You did your part. God will give me the sight."

The next day was Sunday. I went to church and said, "I could not see anything even though the surgery is done. Let's pray." We prayed, and a week later I was able to see. So thank God, I was able to see.

The doctor said, "It's been one week that you've been able to see, but you still need to have good sight, and we need to operate on your other eye." The same lady checked me and said no blood test was needed.

After the second operation, I wasn't able to see with the other eye. I said, "Lord, now I can see with the right eye very well. You have to do something." Within a week, I was able to see much better, even better than the right eye. I was able to get my driver's license, which the doctor had suspended before the surgery because of my vision.

Everyone came and encouraged me not to be afraid of surgery.

I was not afraid of surgery. I'm not afraid of pain. I'm not afraid of suffering. The only thing is that I never went to a doctor at all, but now I understood. Just like you're going to get a haircut and you go to a barber, or you want to cut your nails and you go to a nail salon, I couldn't take cataracts out myself, and so I went somewhere where the cataracts could be taken out.

Only God gives eyesight, and God proved it to me. Even though the surgery was done, the doctor could not give me sight. God gave me sight. God gave me much better sight than I had before. I don't need any other glasses. So God has done mighty things.

ten

✼

TRIPS TO RUSSIA AND TEXAS

God brought me to the USA to preach the gospel around the world, and He made it possible with the printed page, internet, and radio programs. I visited many states in the USA. At the same time, I was always looking for an opportunity to go to different countries and preach the gospel. God gave me an opportunity to go to Russia with the Trinity Broadcasting Network, and later I visited TBN in Texas.

TRIP TO RUSSIA

One hundred and twenty people were going from the USA to Russia. I called the group that was going, and God provided everything in due time for me to go with them. The trip was arranged by Dr. Paul Crouch, the founder and president of TBN, and so I felt very secure, going with the children of God. The year was 1992, and Russia had a lot of problems at that particular time. I thought that the door to go to Russia might close, and I made sure not to miss this trip.

Someone arranged for a limousine to take me to the airport.

The limousine driver parked across the street because he was going in another direction. While he was keeping my bag in the luggage compartment, I ran across the street and opened the limousine door in a hurry. Somehow I hit my head very hard against the door. It was hurting so much that my eyes watered and my face swelled, but somehow I sat in my seat and prayed that God should take away my pain and that I would not have any clot or bleeding. (I still have a dent in my head, to this day.)

I was praying and quietly sitting there. One passenger sitting beside me began to get nervous and panicked. She said, "This limousine is getting late, and I have a connecting flight, and if I don't go on time, everything will be a problem." She was almost crying.

I said to her, "I'm going to pray for you, and you will have a safe journey. You will have a connecting flight, and you will meet whomever is coming to meet you. Everything will be all right. Would you please send me a postcard when God hears our prayer?"

She said, "Okay, surely I'll do that."

Thank God, when I prayed for that sister, forgetting my own pain, God took away my pain, and I felt better. (When I returned home, her postcard was already waiting for me, and she thanked God that her prayer was answered.)

When I was in the plane, there was one lady sitting beside me, and she had a severe stomach ache. She was asking if someone could give her something for her stomach.

I said, "Sister, do you believe that God can heal your stomach ache?"

"Yes," she said.

"I'm going to pray for you," I said. "Put your hand on your stomach, and let's pray." I prayed in the name of Jesus, and instantly her pain was gone. I was praising and thanking God.

We reached St. Petersburg, and we were lining up, waiting for our hotel room. I was praying that I would have a good roommate at our hotel. I had never shared a room with anyone before. I ended up sharing a room with one brother from Georgia. He was very nice, godly and humble. He was also an airplane mechanic and pilot.

After we got to our room, he asked me, "Are you a pastor?"

"Yes," I said.

"Why don't you pray for me?" he asked.

"You never asked me to pray," I said. "If you ask me, I will pray. I don't know what is your prayer request."

"I have a severe headache," he said. "My head is splitting. I took a shower a couple of times and washed my head with cold water, but the pain is not going."

I said, "Do you want me to lay hands on your head and pray?"

"Yes," he said.

I laid hands and prayed in the name of Jesus. I rebuked that headache, and instantly, the headache was gone. So this brother was very happy, and he told all of his friends what God did.

I was testifying to this brother, and he was listening quietly, very much interested in my testimony. I don't know how many hours we were talking, but time went so fast. It was almost evening now, and the buses had already left for the crusade at the big stadium in Moscow. When I looked at my watch, I said, "Don't you know we have to go for that meeting?"

This brother said, "The bus has already left."

I said, "I have to go there, because God can use me there."

"Don't worry," he said. "We'll take a taxi."

We called a taxi, but we didn't know the language or the address of the stadium. We told the taxi driver to take us to the biggest stadium, and he took us there without a problem. When we went there, the stadium was filled with people, and the meeting was in progress.

In the middle of the service, one brother came and whispered in my ear, "Pastor Peter, there are two Russian boys who are deaf and dumb. I want you to pray for them. I know God can hear your prayer."

I said, "If I pray for them right now, they're going to get healed and make a lot of noise. Their parents, their friends and all the people will start running toward them, and it will be a disturbance to the service. Could you please wait until the service is over? As soon as the stage lights are off, I'll pray for them."

He agreed, and in the meantime, I was praying in my heart that God should do some miracle.

As soon as the stage lights were off, this brother brought those boys and their parents. One boy was about twelve years old, and the other was about ten. I prayed for them in the name of Jesus and rebuked that deafness and dumbness. All of a sudden, those children started talking.

I said to them, "Say 'Jesus.'"

They said, "Jesus."

I said, "Praise the Lord."

They started saying, "Praise the Lord."

They could hear, and they could talk. I was so thankful to God, and, exactly as I had said, people started rushing toward us and telling me to pray for them.

The next morning, we were having breakfast at the hotel. Dr. Crouch came with his wife and asked the people, "Are you people having fun?"

Everybody said, "Yes."

One brother stood and said, "In that stadium, there were two boys, deaf and dumb. Pastor Peter prayed for them, and they began speaking and hearing."

Dr. Crouch said, "Who is that pastor?"

So I stood, and he just said, "Praise the Lord."

God started using me in Russia, and Russian people started coming to the hotel and asking me to pray for them.

There was a Russian Pentecostal church with four thousand members. Dr. Crouch was invited to speak there, and he told them he would be coming. We took buses to attend the service, and people there were singing and praising God, waiting for Dr. Crouch to come. Half an hour later, he called the pastor and said that he would be late because he and his wife were giving toys to children at an orphanage.

I gave my card to an usher and told him, "This is my card. Give it to your pastor and tell him I'm available to speak." So the usher gave the card to the pastor. The pastor just took the card, did not even read it, and put it in his pocket.

After a while, Dr. Crouch called and said that he might not be coming. Finally, he called again and said that he was not coming. When the pastor heard that Dr. Crouch was not coming, he took the card out of his pocket, read it, and asked if I was still available.

I said, "Yes, sir."

So he called me to the stage. Now, it was getting late, and people were getting tired. I told them, "I know you are very tired. I will not take much time, but I will give a short message. After the message, I will pray for you." When I finished preaching, I said to the congregation, "I am going to pray for your healing, if anyone is sick. I am not telling anyone to come to the stage, because time is very short. I am going to do a general prayer for everyone. I believe that God is going to hear the prayer, and everyone is going to be healed."

I said to the people standing there, "Touch your hand on your body, wherever you need prayer, head or chest or whatever, and I'll pray for you." Many people did that, and God healed them. Many people came to shake my hand, but the buses were leaving. So I just ran to the bus and went back to the hotel. However, many of these people came to the hotel. They were asking me to pray for them or telling people about how God healed them. The people were there until midnight, and a security guard came and told the people that, if they were not staying at the hotel, they had to leave, because they were closing the doors.

The next morning, I went down to the hallway and saw that

many people had come back for prayer. One lady had a problem with her bladder. While I was about to pray for her, another lady standing there told me to wait. She said, "Pastor Peter, I'm part of the group that came from America. I had a bladder problem, and I said, 'How can I go to Russia, when I have this problem?' God told me that he would heal me in Russia. I believed that, and I came here. I was listening to your message yesterday in that church. When you prayed for people, I also received my healing, and my problem is completely gone. I am completely healed. So I just wanted to testify to this lady that God healed me. The same God can heal her."

I laid hands and prayed for that lady, and that lady got healed. Every day, people were coming for prayer, and God was healing them.

God did miracles wherever I went. Every day, I went out in the street and talked to people. I took the train from St. Petersburg to Moscow and gave tracts to people, because I had taken many tracts and pamphlets from home to give out to people. I didn't have an interpreter with me, but I just prayed that somebody would know a little bit of English so that I could talk to them. God gave me grace to pray for those people, and many people were very interested in our ministry.

I started giving to Russian people almost all of the cash I had. I didn't need money, because my meals, ticket and limousine were already paid, and so I wasn't worried about finishing my money. However, the word of God says, "Give, and it shall be given unto you" (Luke 6:38). I prayed for many Americans, and they were thankful. They would shake my hand and put money in my hand. When we came together for lunch or dinner, God would inspire some people to give me envelopes containing money. I thanked them and prayed for them. God gave me more money than I had taken with me to Russia.

When you are really dedicated to the Lord, He will open new doors for you. You should always be ready to serve the Lord. Do you see what the devil tried to do? The devil didn't want me to go to Russia, and that's why I got hurt. If I would have told someone that I got hurt in the limousine, they would not even allow me to travel, but I did not tell anyone. I just prayed to God, and God healed me.

TRIP TO TEXAS

TBN was having a celebration, because they had built their new International Production Center. Inside the building was a replica of the upper room where the disciples of Jesus received the Holy Spirit on the day of Pentecost. I decided to go there, and I believed that God would use me there. They had a baptism service, and I taught many people about baptism and prepared them for the service. I met many people in the hotel, ministered to them, and made many friends.

In the meantime, one brother came to know that I was in Texas. He had attended our services when he was in Philadelphia. He called me and said, "Pastor Peter, why are you living in a hotel? Please come and stay with me." He sent his son to pick me up in a Cadillac. He also arranged some services in his house for me to conduct.

"Pastor Peter, my son will be your driver," he said. "He will take you wherever you want to go."

I told him that I wanted to go back to the International Production Center. When I came, there was a celebration going on, but I just wanted to see the upper room. I went up and saw one woman sitting there and praying. She was about sixty years old. I touched her shoulder and said, "I'm sorry to interrupt your prayer, but I'm going to pray with you, because Matthew 18:19 says that if two people agree touching anything, God will hear their prayer. So I'm going to add my faith to yours, and we will pray together. God will answer our prayer. Could you tell me what is your prayer request?"

She said, "I am a born again believer. Since I was born again, I was asking God to fill me with the Holy Spirit with the evidence of speaking in tongues."

I laid hands and prayed that God would give her the Holy Spirit. As soon as I prayed for her, right away she received the Holy Spirit and started speaking in tongues.

I went back to the house, because I had another service to conduct there. I think the homeowner's son, who was my driver, might have told his parents about what happened in the upper room, because his father said to me, "My wife doesn't have the Holy Spirit. She doesn't speak in tongues. I'm planning to start a church in Texas, and I want my wife to be filled with the Holy Spirit. Could you please pray for her?"

I said, "We will have a service tonight, and afterward I will pray for your wife."

That night, I gave a Bible study about the Holy Spirit. After the service, I said, "If anyone wants to receive the Holy Spirit, please come, and I will pray for you." His wife came forward, and I laid hands and prayed for her to receive the Holy Spirit. God filled her with the Holy Spirit, with the evidence of speaking in tongues, and she and her husband were very happy. Afterward, God did a miracle, and he started his own church.

He said, "I have another prayer request. I have another house, but there is no tenant coming to rent it. Could you please pray that somebody will come and rent my house?"

I said, "Let's pray." We prayed, and as soon as I said, "Amen," the phone rang. So I said, "Pick up that phone. That is the person who is going to rent your building."

The man who called was an assistant pastor at an Assemblies of God church. I said, "Brother, see how God is great. You don't have to worry for your rent, because this man is a man of God, and he will give the rent on time."

God wants us to be willing vessels. God can use anyone. If someone is a born again child of God, God has given us authority over demonic forces. Please read 1 John 4:4: "Greater is he that is in you, than he that is in the world." Jesus already said in John 14:12, "He that believeth on me, the works that I do shall he do also; and greater works than these shall he do." So I believe that since 1956 until today, God has done signs and wonders and miracles in my ministry. I'm saying this so that anyone can say, "If God can use this ordinary man, God can use me." There is nothing impossible with God. St. Paul says in Philippians 4:13, "I can do all things through Christ which strengtheneth me." From these verses, we can see that there is also nothing impossible for the child of God.

Wherever you go, start from your home and say, "Lord, I'm going in Your Name. If I see somebody is in trouble and needs prayer or my counseling, give me grace to minister to them." God will inspire you in the right time and guide you in what to do.

In this book, I tried to tell you what God has done in my life. If I try to tell you everything, I will not have room in this book. However, I just wanted to let you know that, wherever you go, if God is with you, God will use you mightily for the glory of God. I have dedicated my life, and I'm going to serve the Lord.

So I invite you to call upon Jesus. Say, "Lord Jesus, come into my heart. Be my Lord. Be my Savior. I give my life to You, and I want to be a useful vessel for You. In Jesus' name I pray. Amen." God will use you for His glory.

May God richly bless you and use you more and more for His glory. Amen.

Printed in the United States
by Baker & Taylor Publisher Services